Advance Praise for *Unlearning the Hush: Oral Histories of Black Female Educators in Mississippi in the Civil Rights Era*

"*Unlearning the Hush* offers fresh perspectives on Black women teachers and the use of oral history as a tool for uncovering hidden histories. Weaving in her own personal experiences as a teacher throughout the book, Bunch's narratives of Black teachers in Mississippi are resonant and compelling for our times. Drawing from the Black intellectual tradition, Bunch's approach utilizes art, poetry, and stories to illuminate histories. This book is masterful, creative, and inspiring."

—Dr. Derrick Alridge, director of the Teachers in the Movement Project, University of Virginia

"Marlee Bunch's *Unlearning the Hush* is a riveting exploration of resilience and activism. Through meticulous research and poignant storytelling, Bunch magnifies the voices of Black women educators, long overshadowed by history's silence. *Unlearning the Hush* is a testament to the strength and determination of those who dared to challenge the status quo. A profound and necessary addition to the annals of educational history, Bunch's work will inspire and enlighten readers for generations to come."

—TJ Jackson, host of The Power of Love Show

"Marlee Bunch's *Unlearning the Hush* presents an urgently needed and elegantly crafted work of oral histories that pays tribute to the lives and legacies of Black female educators; by bringing their voices and their stories to life on the page, Bunch elevates these historical narratives in ways that connect deeply to our current cultural and societal moment, calling us to listen to the past so that we can fight for a more equitable and inclusive future. A rich text for educators and students alike, this book fills a curricular gap—and will open opportunities for learning nationwide.

—Brittany R. Collins, author of *Learning from Loss: A Trauma-Informed Approach to Supporting Grieving Students*

"One of the most revered opportunities of librarianship is the moment we connect seekers, readers, researchers, and naysayers to life-changing books. When we ourselves finish books that light us up from the inside, we scramble to tell the people we love, and we wait in delight for the moment we are approached with a request that aligns with the book's breadth and intent. We gain our composure in these moments, of course, remembering our recommendations carry weight; but there is no better feeling than whispering, "you have to read this book!" *Unlearning the Hush* is one of those books for me. It is a testimony to the power of classrooms and an ode to black educators—past, present, and future."

—Angel Tucker, Johnson County Library, Overland Park, Kansas

Unlearning the Hush

TRANSFORMATIONS: WOMANIST, FEMINIST,
AND INDIGENOUS STUDIES

Edited by AnaLouise Keating

*For a list of books in the series, please see
our website at www.press.uillinois.edu.*

Unlearning the Hush

Oral Histories of Black Female Educators in Mississippi in the Civil Rights Era

MARLEE S. BUNCH

Foreword by
CHRISTOPHER M. SPAN

© 2025 by the Board of Trustees
of the University of Illinois
All rights reserved
Manufactured in the United States of America
1 2 3 4 5 C P 5 4 3 2 1
♾ This book is printed on acid-free paper.

Cover image: Kevin Hopkins, *Mother I Graduated*, 2022.
Artwork is made on fabric with cyanotypes of photographs.
Photographs are a collage of Hattiesburg images, images
of the author's family, and images of the artist's family.
Also included is a photo of Mrs. Zola Jackson, educator.
Courtesy of the artist.

Cataloging data available from the Library of Congress

ISBN 9780252046766 (hardcover)
ISBN 9780252088872 (paperback)
ISBN 9780252048319 (ebook)

To the women and educators of Mississippi who refused to be hushed or silenced, and their students who carried forward their lessons

For Bella, Townes, and Aiden

May you always remember our stories and history, and may the strength of these inspire you

Kevin Hopkins, *Mother I Graduated*, 2022. Artwork is made on fabric with cyanotypes of photographs. Photographs are a collage of Hattiesburg images, images of the author's family, and images of the artist's family.

Dedication

This narrative is dedicated to the many people who have influenced my life. First and foremost, I want to honor and remember my grandmom Marian—I hope I have made you proud. I dedicate this work to my grandmothers, Victoria, and Momma. All of you were formative in shaping who I am and how I regard memory, stories, strong women, and the sense of home. You are everything that connects my past and present, and I am eternally in awe of the women you are. I aspire to be like you every single day. Thank you, always and forever.

I dedicate this to all Black women: we share a vast strength and wisdom.

I dedicate this to Emmett Till and to the many others who lost their lives by violence.

I dedicate this to my students.

I dedicate this to my family and friends.

I dedicate this to my children—you are everything.

I dedicate this to my elders and ancestors.

I dedicate this to all Black educators in Hattiesburg and beyond who created possibilities.

Through this act of remembering, I honor our history and all of you. I celebrate my ancestors who overcame so much to allow me to be here, and I celebrate the generational blessings and stories that remain to be told.

they ask me to remember
but they want me to remember
their memories
and I keep on remembering mine

—Lucille Clifton, "why some people
   be mad at me sometimes"

Contents

Companion Website xiii
Visual Art and Poets xiv
Series Foreword by AnaLouise Keating. xvi
Foreword by Christopher M. Span xix
Poetic Reflection by Ariana Benson xxi
Preface and Origin Story xxiii
Acknowledgments. xxxiii
Poetic Reflection by Mary Ruefle xxxv

CHAPTER 1. "Everybody Knows about Mississippi" 1
  Poetic Reflection by Evie Shockley. 2
  Historical Vignette by Christopher M. Span 9
  Poetic Reflection by Ariana Benson 12
CHAPTER 2. The Wisdom of Elders 13
  Poetic Reflection by Emily Pettit. 14
  Historical Vignette by Christopher M. Span 74
  Poetic Reflection by Nate Marshall. 77
CHAPTER 3. Unwavering Determination. 80
  Poetic Reflection by Jordan Stempleman 81
  Historical Vignette by Christopher M. Span 88
  Poetic Reflection by Maxine Chernoff. 91

CHAPTER 4. Love Is Resistance 92
   Poetic Reflection by Cole Swensen............................ 93
   Historical Vignette by Christopher M. Span 107
   Poetic Reflection by Stanley Banks........................... 110

CHAPTER 5. Legacies and Artifacts............................. 112
   Poetry Reflection by Ashley M. Jones 113
   Historical Vignette by Christopher M. Span 128
   Poetic Reflection by Jordan Stempleman 130

EPILOGUE: Listening to the Lessons............................ 131
   Poetic Reflection by Claudia Rankine 134
   Audio Poems Narrated by Ashley M. Jones 138
   Poetic Reflection by Michelle Taransky 140

Abbreviations and People List 143
Notes 145
Bibliography 153
Index 175

Companion Website

Readers of *Unlearning the Hush* are invited to visit the supplemental materials found at the University of Illinois Press website and accessed through the web page for the book. The site contains selected audio clips relevant to the text.

Visual Art and Poets

Visual Art

Since collaborating with visual artist Kevin Hopkins for an art exhibit related to this research that we co-curated at HAW Contemporary Gallery in 2022, I knew the important element that art would add to this research and book, as it complemented the themes and history. Good Black Art collaborated and shared communication with their artists to help me find artists and artwork that would correlate with the book. I chose artists whose artwork I admire and that fit well with each chapter. All visual artists are BIPOC individuals (Black/Indigenous/People of Color). In addition, three artists (Kevin Hopkins, Kevin Demery, Hùng Lê) are all local artists in my hometown of Kansas City. All visual artists were invited to submit visual artwork that they felt connected with the themes of the book. Phillip Collins, Founder of Good Black Art (where many of the visual artists in the book have showcased their artwork), shared these thoughts when asked about the connections between art, history, and oral histories: "In a world where histories, experiences, and stories are at risk of erasure, it is crucial to document our truths today. History continues to unfold daily, irrespective of age, education, or background, creating a profound sense of urgency to safeguard it. We encourage our community, both inside and outside of the art ecosystem, to broaden the definition of 'collecting art' and to embrace the role of guardians of artists' legacies. By amplifying their voices through the timeless medium of books, we aim to create a lasting impact on the preservation of their narratives."

Poems

The poems featured in this book are all written by established and esteemed poets whom I have admired for many years. Though a diverse group of poets is featured, most are female, again celebrating the female participants in the text. The poets were asked to share existing poems or to write new poems that connected to the themes of the book. For example, poems by Ariana Benson deal with historical references and the South, while "Haint Blue" by Cole Swensen deals with the legend that painting one's porch a "haint" blue color kept ghosts away. "Lessons" by Jordan Stempleman and "Miss Banks" by Maxine Chernoff were written especially for this book, while others were published here for the first time (for example, poems by Michelle Taransky and Ashley M. Jones). The University of Illinois Press website contains links to a reading that features some of the poems in the book, read by Ashley M. Jones. This can be accessed through the supplemental material tab on the book page. The poems specifically are meant to allow the content from each chapter to linger, opening up potential areas of reflection and contemplation. This is where we find moments that allow us to better appreciate stories and expansive history not often voiced.

Poets Included in This Book

Stanley Banks
Ariana Benson
Maxine Chernoff
Ashley M. Jones
Nate Marshall
Emily Pettit
Claudia Rankine
Mary Ruefle
Evie Shockley
Jordan Stempleman
Cole Swensen
Michelle Taransky

Visual Artists Included in This Book

Aliyah Bonnette
André Chung
Kevin Demery
Andrew Feiler
Kevin Hopkins
Mario Joyce
Hùng Lê
Rebecca Marimutu
Utē Petit

Series Foreword

> This book is an ode to Black women, educators, mentors, and ancestors. It is a quilt of voices and stories. These oral histories, accounts, and stories are for future generations, future educators to document that we are here, and erasure will never diminish the greatness of our stories. To understand the magnitude of our stories is to better comprehend our vast beauty.
> —Dr. Marlee S. Bunch

What does transformation look like? How can language, reading, writing, education, and storytelling empower us to enact progressive social change? How can we use words, ideas, theories, and stories to develop inclusive, life-affirming communities? What tools can assist us as we work to enact this transformation in our daily practices, our classrooms, and other areas of life? *Transformations: Womanist, Feminist, & Indigenous Studies* has its origins in these and related questions. Grounded in the belief that radical progressive change—on individual, collective, national, transnational, and planetary levels—is urgently needed and in fact possible (although typically not easy to achieve), this book series exists to create new pathways for transdisciplinary scholarship informed by women-of-colors theories and post-oppositional approaches to knowledge creation and social change. *Transformations* invites authors to take risks (thematically, theoretically, methodologically, and/or stylistically) in their work—to draw on existing knowledge systems while, simultaneously, moving beyond these systems and their disciplinary—or interdisciplinary—specific academic rules; through these risks, authors in this series invent new (transdisciplinary) perspectives, methods, and knowledge. Books in this series foreground women-of-colors theorizing and perspectives because they offer boldly innovative, though too often overlooked, insights and models for transformation. Women-of-colors theories give us the intellectual grounding and visionary-yet-pragmatic tools to understand, challenge, and alter the existing frameworks and paradigms that structure (and, all too often, constrain) our lives. They are more daring, innovative, and imaginative ... rich with the potential to transform.

Unlearning the Hush: Oral Histories of Black Female Educators in Mississippi in the Civil Rights Era beautifully illustrates this daring, innovative potential. It reminds us that profound transformation can occur through focused determination, steady self-confidence, and the willingness to honor and learn from our past. This book showcases the voices and perspectives of Black educators (primarily women) who worked in Jim Crow Mississippi, at a time when silence was inscribed into law and imposed through segregated spaces, constant surveillance, and many other unjust practices. Despite the genuine risks of physical, psychic, and psychological violence, these educators were not silent; they used their voices strategically, to build community and effect change. Thanks to Dr. Bunch's diligent, inspired efforts, their memories, perspectives, and stories live on. Their words empower us, urging us to carry their wisdom forward.

This book is profoundly collaborative and multiplicitous. It includes historical vignettes (Bunch's term to describe the complex historical layering she employs), poetry, photographs, artwork, letters to future generations, and first-person accounts from educators and students. By gathering this wide variety of firsthand memories and experiences, Bunch expands the historical record in vital ways. In documenting these stories through her painstaking, thoughtful work, Bunch highlights them and supports their endurance. She looks, simultaneously, back to the past (recording the oral histories) and forward into the future (inviting participants to share messages for the next generations). In so doing, she enacts "Sankofa"—a word from the Akan people of Ghana that underscores the importance of reflecting on the past in order to build a better future. Or, as contributor Mrs. Linda Armstrong puts it, Sakofa instructs us to "go back and get it." This book looks back at a past that we must not forget and, simultaneously, encourages us to take history's lessons forward; we must use these historical lessons to build an inclusive future in which all children (and adults) can thrive.

Contributors to this volume remind us that education is incredibly powerful. In the brilliant words of Mrs. Ellie Davis Dahmer: "Remember the slave owner could beat a slave, rape a slave, abuse a slave in any manner, sell a slave away from their family and it wasn't against the law. It was only illegal to educate a slave." Education liberates. May we activate education's liberatory potential.

I am so delighted to include *Unlearning the Hush* in the Transformations book series. This book is a love song. A labor of love about Black southern educators, primarily women, who labored *for* love—love of students, love of family, love of self, love of race, love of education. Contributors provide commonsense wisdom forged through experience. To offer only a few of these important reminders:

- "As you climb, take others with you."—Mrs. Mary Bobbitt
- "Education is never over with. There are always things you can learn."—Eleanor Dolores Goins
- "Library cards are free. Get one. Use it. Reading is the basis for further education."—Mrs. Ellie Davis Dahmer
- "Embrace your inner self. There is a little voice inside all of us, and it speaks to us. No matter what is happening in the external world around you, always listen to that voice. Never silence your inner voice, because it is there for a reason, emerging from your subconscious. Listen to your internal monologue and learn to love yourself."—Dr. Joyce A Ladner

May we inscribe their wisdom on our hearts. May we deeply remember and learn from the memories and experiences contained within these pages. May we use these insights to nourish education's profound potential.

AnaLouise Keating

Foreword

Reflecting on this important book reveals a wealth of invaluable lessons, with the foremost lesson revolving around history itself.

History, far from being a linear narrative with a clear beginning, middle, and end, is a complex tapestry woven from fragmented pieces of evidence. Within this tapestry lie stories of triumph and heroism, stories that illuminate the human spirit in the face of adversity. The true power of this book lies in its ability to uncover these narratives.

Dr. Marlee Bunch's courageous endeavor to ask pivotal questions of the teachers and elders she has interviewed encapsulates the essence of this undertaking. Many of these stories reside within the minds of individuals who have accomplished remarkable feats—some might even say extraordinary deeds. Yet, the only way to unlock these narratives is by asking the right questions: How did you do it? Why did you do it?

Unlearning the Hush delves into the heart of what every community should contemplate: Why do we do what we do? Why do we care for the communities we serve? And how do we persevere in the face of daunting challenges and societal constraints? This book encapsulates the power of these inquiries, revealing the resilience and determination of the Black teachers of Hattiesburg, Mississippi, who have dedicated themselves to their communities.

By examining the motivations and challenges faced by these individuals, Bunch sheds light on the intricacies of their experiences. How did they navigate through life's obstacles, Jim Crow, and the pressures of complying with *Brown*? What compelled them to serve their communities with such dedication? These questions unveil a deeper understanding of

African American history, one that transcends conventional narratives and embraces the richness of lived experiences.

Indeed, the stories contained within this book defy traditional modes of storytelling. They echo the call and response tradition ingrained in African American culture, where every voice contributes to a collective narrative. Through oral histories and shared wisdom, these stories offer invaluable insights that resonate with our present reality.

For educators and policy makers, the lessons gleaned from these narratives are particularly poignant. The education of African American children holds immense significance, as it shapes the trajectory of their futures. The teachers of Hattiesburg knew this all too well. Within these pages lie not only lessons but also a roadmap for action—a blueprint for creating meaningful change in our contemporary educational systems.

Ultimately, the purpose of understanding the past is to inform our present decisions and guide our future endeavors. As we embark on this journey through history, let us heed the lessons contained within these pages. Let us honor the resilience and wisdom of those who came before us by striving to create a more just and equitable society for generations to come. Let us thank Dr. Marlee Bunch for taking the time to attentively listen, "un-hush," and document the histories of these Black female educators in Hattiesburg, Mississippi.

Christopher M. Span

POETIC REFLECTION

Elders Speak of the Windchimes[1]

Ariana Benson

that quivered in the maples, the poplars, the hollowed pipes, their coppered shine in the gloaming, some notched with patterns as if by potter's curved blade, some filled to the mouth with birdseed and monkshood, as if to lure the crows and hornets and citrus swallowtails— and so they came, pitch-hued and thick as locusts—

some intoned a song that followed elders everywhere: on the smoked-out bus, in the old vine-mangled lean-to, past the corner store, resounding through the sundown valleys, through the tobacco leaves, a sour sound, like the ringing in your teeth after the first bite of an underripe nectarine, it became the score of their dreams, that chimesong;

chimes made of bloodwet Stone Mountain clay and kiln-fired Gullah mud, chimes those icy gales withered to bone, chimes that sung all alone without other chimes to strike, to crack their sorrow against, and louder, still, than the solo chimes, were the chimes that had others alongside them, others with whom to lift that flickering din heavenward: that soprano trill that could be heard over the midnight crickets, over even the thunderous Sunday organs, over the caterwauling sinnermen, over the rejoicing

"Tete ka asom ene Kakyere."
Ancient things remain in the ear.
—Akan Ghanian proverb

Kevin Hopkins, *Momma*, 2022. Cyanotype, acrylic paint, and fabric. A former student of the author looks on at the painting during an art exhibit at HAW Contemporary Gallery.

Preface and Origin Story

> There are years that ask questions
> and years that answer.
> —Zora Neale Hurston

My story is embedded within the stories of educators who came before me, ancestors, and strong Black women whose lives brought forth the possibilities for mine. When I was young my grandmother would write me a little note and place it in my brown paper lunch bag each day. She did this from first grade through most of middle school. Those letters bridged generations, growing pains, adolescent angst, and everything in between—they were the opening pieces of my story and my first exposure to the power that stories hold. While I was growing up, stories became a way to keep memories alive, a way to remember. These stories and the women around me gave me my sense of home and taught me to value listening to the stories and words of others. This allowed both my grandmother and Momma to instill a sense of the world and history in me.

My career path as an educator would put me in learning spaces with students who desired relevant learning, connection, and mentorship. Our classroom would become a place to cultivate the histories of others, one that allowed us to use stories to learn and connect. These stories served as a vehicle to help students analyze texts, write poems, self-reflect, understand their identity, and build relationships. The stories of the past and present would become the backdrop to my classroom. Documenting each other's journeys, our stories would merge to create new possibilities within these histories and shared experiences.

These experiences would lead me to this moment and place. The merging of my teaching, my history, the women who have affirmed and uplifted, and the reflections of community members—they are all interwoven in this book. I am a conduit of stories to remember, document, and pass on. Ultimately, we all are. If there is any remedy or certain answer for making our world better, it most certainly begins with the histories bound up in stories and the act of listening and reclaiming these memories.

Significance

> That's what memory does . . . It allows a living community to shape its past in profound ways.
> —Secretary Lonnie Bunch, Interview, October 2021

While I was searching for the words to summarize the significance of this book, nothing quite encapsulated it until I came across the above quote by Lonnie Bunch, a historian and the Secretary of the Smithsonian Institution. His quote represents this research, as this book is a collective endeavor, a community approach toward preserving and capturing oral histories, stories, lived experiences, memories, and artifacts.

Relying extensively on oral history, this book details the lived experiences and voices of Black female educators, specifically those who taught in Hattiesburg, Mississippi before and after *Brown v. Board of Education*, the landmark 1954 U.S. Supreme Court decision. Ever present is the fact that Black female teachers, despite the challenges they endured, remained steadfast in shining their light for their students caught in the crossfire of undoing centuries of segregation policy and practice.

This book and the documentation of these histories attempt to undo the hush that has silenced or unacknowledged these women in the historical record. It is an attempt to reclaim the names and oral histories integral to Black history. Far too often, the voices of Black women have been disregarded, questioned, discounted, or silenced. Notwithstanding, since the Emancipation Proclamation was issued in 1863, Black women as educators have been at the forefront of ensuring Black students and communities were given the civil liberty of education and literacy. Throughout history, these educators found creative ways to navigate, and periodically upend, systemic practices in American society that legally or purposefully sought to deny Black folk their personhood, education, and access to full-fledged citizenship. The efforts of these educators not only preserved and enhanced Black life and opportunity, but they also forever changed the laws and landscape of the United States by challenging the expectations that were imposed on Black students and affirming those students both in and out of the classroom.[2]

While in recent years we have been offered a robust amount of literature that discusses the role of Black educators and the history of Black education (e.g., Vanessa Siddle Walker, Christopher M. Span, James Anderson,

Adam Fairclough, and others), we have little that focuses specifically on Hattiesburg, Mississippi educators.[3] Decades of silence have created the need to center the experiences of Black women and correct the imbalance of the weight of history. Amplifying the voices of these women, who were trailblazers in their profession and craft, serves as a corrective to the underinclusion and underemphasis of the role Black female teachers in Mississippi played in the desegregation efforts to dismantle Jim Crow schools.[4]

Central to this narrative are my grandmother and my mother. My mother attended segregated Black schools within the Hattiesburg school system her entire life. My grandmother was an educator and community leader who, alongside other Black women of Hattiesburg, found ways to ensure the Black school experience there was exceptional.[5] The voices of past educators guide this text and provide glimpses into the valuable contributions they made to their students, classrooms, and communities. Their stories serve as a foundation for others to share these histories, making known the actual people who changed lives and advocated for dismantling unjust systems.

As you delve into this book, you will see that stories and histories intertwine, blending oral history and the creation of artifacts. Stories are not singular, and the overlapping of voices illustrates the connection of the past and present. While the body of research regarding Black educators is thankfully growing, there is still much to document. These intimate glimpses into the interior lives of educators and students who navigated segregation and desegregation in Hattiesburg Public Schools and Forrest County Public Schools offer their own voice perspectives for understanding this important history. Having a myriad of voices in conjunction with participants who were educators allowed for perspective and depth, and interviewing past educators, students of past educators, and historians allowed a full picture of these histories to emerge. While this research focuses primarily on Black women, it in no way diminishes the valuable contributions made by Black male educators throughout history. Additionally, hearing from the students of the educators in this study offers valuable insights, solidifying the efforts and investment that educators were making in the classroom, and confirming their dedication to their students and community.

I chose to create a more intimate and immersive study, which was achieved by conducting in-depth interviews with each participant, including extended follow-up questions and communication. Interviews were conducted with the following four understandings: (1) not all Mississippi schools and educators had the same circumstances as Hattiesburg, with its effective schools and educators; (2) not all Hattiesburg Black educators were equal in expertise or impact; (3) Jim Crow laws and entrenched racial and systemic inequities permeated Mississippi, including Hattiesburg; and (4) the promise of *Brown* and desegregation was regarded as hopeful; the tension between implementing and staving off desegregation was what many participants in this book found problematic.

Participants shared insights of their whole self, which included recollections of childhood, stories of school days, positive memories, the joys and struggles of teaching, and so forth. Therefore, let us consider the counter-narrative and bear witness to the perspectives of participants as we work to expand the historical record and listen to those who lived this history.

My grandmother's memories are interlaced with the stories of her affinity for classical music, her love of poetry, and her deep appreciation for literature—parts of herself that she would share with her students. My mother followed in her footsteps, continuing this tradition—when she was growing up, my mother would stand by the kitchen window, reciting poems she had written. These moments in their histories are part of a long-standing connection to written and visual art.

As remarkable as the oral histories found in this book are, the artwork that complements and enhances the stories is just as powerful. Art embodies so many emotions and vulnerabilities that sometimes elude us, and it facilitates opportunities for connection, bringing stories and humanity to the forefront. Good Black Art, led by Phillip Collins, is an online art space that features artwork from emerging and established Black artists such as Mario Joyce, Kevin Hopkins, Rebecca Marimutu, and others from across the globe as they use their craft to tell stories and create spaces for learning and community engagement. Featured in the following pages are poets and visual artists whose work aligns with the history and stories of the participants. Artistic and intellectual approaches via writing and other forms of art were used historically not only as a form of self-expression but also to document and record what was occurring in society and history. This tradition embodies the vastness of Black culture regarding the intersection of art, writing, and the oral tradition. From the poetry of Phillis Wheatley to the storytelling found in quilts, the artwork in this book, and more, art has always been embedded in Black history. This expansive view creates inroads for you (the reader) to experience each poem and visual art piece, threading this tradition throughout the book, and immersing you in the stories of participants. As you experience each poem and visual art piece, I invite you to pause, consider what you've read, reflect, and connect.

One of the first books that left a lasting impression on me was Zora Neale Hurston's *Their Eyes Were Watching God*. The title *Unlearning the*

Hush was inspired by the sentiments in Hurston's novel and the idea that you must work toward using your voice. In the story, the main character, Janie, goes on a journey to discover her self-identity. "Unlearning the hush" begins with dismantling the silencing that society often imposes on Black women and Black history. The phrase is an important component of this book, as it speaks to shaking off constructs imposed on marginalized people through systemic and structural racism. It is an ever-present reminder to honor past legacies by building on the difficult work and efforts of those who came before and using our voices to disrupt systems and practices that perpetuate inequities.

Conversations with participants allowed me to further understand this concept of hushed and/or unhushed. For example, Dr. Joyce Ladner shared that her generation was not hushed, as they felt a responsibility to be changemakers, particularly after the murder of young Emmett Till. Speaking up, protesting, or advocating for equal rights could result in being fired, jailed, beaten, or murdered. However, participants were willing to do so to advocate for justice. The contributors to this book all raised their voices to advocate for a better and more equitable tomorrow.

Henry Glassie, professor and author, said it well: "Disorderly, fragmentary, malleable history leaves room for diverse participation. The professionals cannot do it perfectly, so all can take a turn. They must. Everyone is obliged by history's cultural importance and its clear use in planning to try at times to pull a little account of the past into order, to act like a historian. Being important and impossible, history remains worth doing and learning."[6] This book is my attempt, as Glassie says, to "pull a little account of the past into order." This book is for everyday people, for scholar-practitioners, and for those interested in better understanding the stories of Black educators and our collective history, by using oral histories as its primary source. The companion teaching guide to this book moves the application of history and oral histories into learning spaces. Titled *The Magnitude of Us: An Educator's Guide to Creating Culturally Responsive Classrooms* (Teachers College Press, Columbia, 2024), the teaching guide allows lessons from this history to move into practice and pedagogy. *Unlearning the Hush* is a journey of tracing stories and history so that we can be empowered to continue building the legacies we were gifted with and better understand ourselves, history, and one another.

The words of Charles Payne in his book *I've Got the Light of Freedom* provided guidance to situate the oral histories in this book against the backdrop of *Brown*. Payne writes, "*Brown* is the kind of Big Event upon which journalists and historians have generally concentrated. . . . The Big Event grew out of a tradition of struggle, that much of the historical initiative was in the hands of the socially obscure, that they were willing to face enormous repressive powers in order to change their world."[7] He goes on to explain that "[t]he inability to convey a sense of process meant that much of what the movement was could not be presented.... The emphasis on what Joyce Ladner calls the 'Big Events' instead of process is particularly distorting."[8] This quote serves as a catalyst for much of this book. Though the "Big Event" of *Brown* is a part of this research, the *process* is about the stories and the collective community efforts that occurred historically, and so it is through that process that this book will attempt to shine a light on the individuals at the center of this history and share this collection of oral histories and recollections with readers.

Life in the Jim Crow South came with not only the realities of violence, segregation, and racism but also the reality that Black communities lived parallel to white communities, as the two were separated by laws. Dr. Joyce Ladner, the sociologist and educator referred to above, tells us that "Black people are involved in a dynamic relationship with their physical and cultural environment in that they both influence it and are influenced by it. This reciprocal relationship allows them to exercise a considerable amount of power over their environs. This also means that they are able to exercise control over their futures...."[9] Without such context, it might be easy to assume that Black communities in the Jim Crow South were *only* marred by violence and struggle. Therefore, it is important to situate the Black community within the reality of a parallel life, allowing readers to understand the both/and of those lived experiences. Black communities and lives were subjected to policies, laws, white supremacy, and systems that were violent and oppressive. However, Black communities *also* found ways to thrive, flourish, excel, and have joy. Despite the impact of outside forces, Black communities created their businesses, processes, institutions, and cultures within these protected spaces (e.g., churches, schools, etc.).[10]

Research has established that Black communities developed ways of operating amid Jim Crow's oppressive laws, as Robin Kelley explains:

> During the era of Jim Crow, black working people carved out social space and constructed what George Lipsitz calls a "culture of opposition" through which to articulate the hidden transcript free from the watchful eye of white authority. African American communities often created an alternative culture emphasizing collectivist values, mutuality, and fellowship. There were vicious, exploitative relationships within southern black communities, particularly across class and gender lines, and the tentacles of Jim Crow touched even black institutions. But the social and cultural institutions and ideologies that ultimately informed black opposition placed more emphasis on communal values and collective

uplift than the prevailing class-conscious, individualist ideology of the white ruling classes. As Earl Lewis so aptly put it, African Americans turned segregation into "congregation."[11]

Research and its contemporary implications highlight the persistent negative impact of white supremacy, emphasizing the historical harm caused by systemic and localized racism—a reality experienced by participants, educators, students, and community members in Hattiesburg and beyond. Simultaneously, the existence of parallel lives provided opportunities for participants to engage with a counternarrative, as explored through the oral histories in chapter 2. Through a strong sense of community and congregation, Black communities were able to thrive and progress within established institutional networks.[12]

My hometown of Kansas City is known for its BBQ. However, one of its BBQ places, Gates BBQ, is different. When you walk in, an employee yells out, "Hi! How may I help you?" Though it's initially jarring, you immediately realize you are somewhere quite different than the other BBQ places. Once inside, you see the subtle, unique details: the textured red glassware, an old coin horse at the front door, tables that look like what one might find in grandma's kitchen, and small white paper cups for BBQ sauce. It's a place for people. It feels familiar and nostalgic. By the time you leave, somehow all its elements make sense, even though it's not a typical restaurant. Sometimes we step into spaces and do not fully understand how to navigate our way until we are fully immersed in them. This book is one of those spaces. As you read it, notice the special features—the poems, the visual art, the artifacts, the letters from participants, and the audio poem option at the end. These elements work together and offer various ways to interact with the content. You can read it from cover to cover or begin your engagement strictly with the art and poetry before listening to the audio poems at the end—it is a book that considers the many ways we learn and reflect.

Readers will notice that this book does not read like a traditional one. Scholarship, in its various forms, should be consistently challenged and reconfigured, and I hope that this research offers a new perspective and approach to this important aspect of history. This book brings to life the voices of Black women who fought for the freedom to be women, educators, mothers, humans, and most of all Black, during a time in our history when the world was not ready to listen. Additionally, a multitude of voices are featured, for two primary reasons: it embodies the spirit of collaboration and collective efforts that participants in this research utilized in their lives, and it offers expertise and perspectives different from my own. Between 2020 and 2024, I interviewed over twenty individuals. They included Black female educators who taught between the 1950s and 1970s, past students who attended Hattiesburg Public Schools between the 1950s and 1970s, a school counselor who worked in Hattiesburg Public Schools, current-day educators, historian and Smithsonian Secretary Lonnie Bunch, who offered insights into the larger historical context, and historian Dr. Christopher M. Span. I invite you, the reader, to pull the lived experiences and stories of participants into your own story. Meaning-making allows us to find our voice, develop interpretations, and blend the experiences of others with the histories we discover, to carry these stories from the page into existence—and to pass them down to others.

Chapter 1 introduces the historical context of desegregation in Mississippi, particularly in Hattiesburg, from the 1950s to the 1970s. Chapter 2 begins the oral histories of the participants, including a photograph of the participant and offering own voice recollections. These primary sources allow readers to experience history through personal accounts and lived experiences. Many of the oral histories end with a personalized letter from the participant to the reader and to future generations, letters that create additional archival documentation of their voices and offer words of affirmation and advice. These letters create an intimate exchange between participants and readers and help continue the tradition of passing down this history. Chapter 3 provides information about the role of the community and the protective spaces where educators leveraged the relationships they built with students and families, and includes information about the schools in Hattiesburg. Chapter 4 overviews and discusses themes that emerged throughout the research and provides additional information from participants. Chapter 5 features additional perspectives from the students of these Hattiesburg teachers and presents rare artifacts (such as annuals and images) shared by participant Charles Cooper. The Epilogue invites us to look ahead and consider how these lessons and stories can inform our actions regarding education today, as we work to enact change. Each chapter includes two poetic reflections, visual art, and a historical vignette by Christopher M. Span. All these elements offer additional context for each chapter, as well as additional historical knowledge. The book's conclusion offers us a sense of hope and reiterates the idea of using our voices. An audible element is included on the supplemental materials link on the University of Illinois Press website book page that invites you to listen to the voice of Ashley M. Jones (poet laureate of Alabama) as she reads some of the poems included in the book, leaving you with the lasting act of engaging directly in the oral tradition. Finally, a multitude of voices and people will be included throughout these chapters to honor and represent the collaboration, community, and mentorship that participants experienced in their own lives.

I hope that reading the oral histories in this book makes you feel something well up inside you, and that it leaves you with an emotional and visceral experience. It is a great responsibility to write the stories of others, one that I approach with the utmost respect, and that means telling this story in a manner that the participants would appreciate; my greatest hope is that this book resonates with the people whom I wrote about, with readers open to new approaches, and with everyday people interested in learning about underrepresented histories. With any luck, this book inspires you, allowing you to recall or embrace past moments. We are all storytellers and keepers of history, and I am grateful to share this history with you.

Mr. Charles Cooper, educator and participant, shared these words with me during the interview process:

> Students and educators in Mississippi found a way—somehow, someway, we found a way to survive and make it. We didn't want to do that, we wanted to instead exist under the idea that all people are created equal, but we knew that wasn't the case. So, we survived and found a way. Our teachers helped us make it. Somehow, someway, teachers found a way to teach us what we needed to know to empower us. Teachers and students knew what they had to do, and they did just that. Separate but equal did not exist, and was not true, so we adjusted and did what we had to do, and the teachers poured their hearts out to us to make it possible. We found a way, and we had moments of joy.[13]

Acknowledging and celebrating women through oral histories is a necessary contribution to the historical record; there should also be an intentional focus on the accomplishments of educators. This does not, of course, come without a deep awareness of the tragedy and violence that occurred in the segregated Jim Crow South, or with a lack of awareness about the struggles Black educators faced in a system not built for us. That is a different story, for a different book.

Black women have not been celebrated enough, certainly not historically, and so while history is part of this book, it is also a celebration of the contributors' lives and the joys that could be cultivated in segregated schools and communities. Celebrations and triumphs are worthy of documentation, especially for Black women, who have been historically and are presently undervalued. Both historical pain and joy are realities the contributors of this book faced. Let us also consider and celebrate the wonders that occurred when Black educators and their students did much with the little that was given to them.

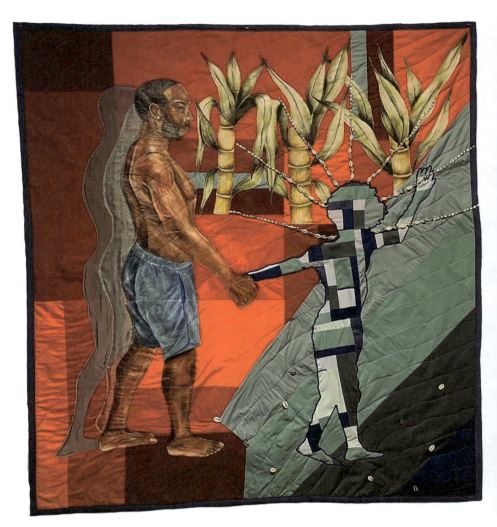

Aliyah Bonnette, *Midnight Rivers*, 2022. Quilt with beading, and applique. "My work is heavily influenced by my relationships with my late grandmothers, my ancestors, or my 'Kindred.' I discovered quilting three years ago after learning that quilting was used in the underground railroad to aid enslaved people to freedom. When I first told my grandfather about my sewing, I learned he had quilts and fabric from my late grandmother. She was a quilter in the 1970s and learned to sew by watching her mother. It was a sign that my grandmothers were alive within me, guiding me all along."

Acknowledgments

The pieces I am, she gathered them and give them right back to me in all the right order.
—Toni Morrison, *Beloved*

This book is an ode to Black women, educators, mentors, and ancestors. It is a quilt of voices and stories. These oral histories, accounts, and stories are for future generations and future educators to document that we were here. Our stories will never be diminished or erased. To understand the magnitude of our stories is to better comprehend our vast beauty.

Though words will never fully express my appreciation and gratitude, I would like to acknowledge the following people:

Grandmom—Thank you for being my sunshine and my role model. Thank you for always supporting me, for loving me wholeheartedly, for encouraging me to do the things that you never got to do and filling my world with unwavering love. Thank you for long car rides, handwritten letters, ice cream days, visits to the library, braiding my hair, and showing me what abounding love looks like. Thank you for teaching me about real truths: unconditional love, appreciating the small things, and the importance of memories. Thank you for every single moment and memory. There is not a day that I do not miss you, and there is not a day that I do not honor you.

Momma—Thank you for your love that has filled my world. Thank you for inspiring me to write, dream, and become. Your belief that I can do anything is the greatest affirmation. Thank you for joy, conversations, and a deep sense of home. I would be lost without your laughter and your love. You are an incredible momma.

Dr. Span—Thank you for being my mentor and kin folk. I went searching for stories of mentorship and excellence, and in my search, I found my mentor in you; for this gift I am ever thankful. Learning from you has been an incredible gift. Thank you for your guidance, time, and encouragement.

To my colleagues at the University of Illinois and Rockhurst University—Thank you for your support and guidance.

Dominique Moore and the team at the University of Illinois Press—Thank you for helping to make these stories visible, and for your support and belief in the vision of this book.

Secretary Lonnie Bunch—Meeting you and having this journey connect our paths has been a true gift. I cannot thank you enough for your kindness, brilliance, and willingness to share your time.

Mr. Cooper, Mrs. Heath, Mrs. Goins, Mrs. Woullard, Mrs. Hale-Green, Dr. Harris, Mrs. Fowler, Mrs. Ellie Dahmer, Ms. Bettie Dahmer, Mrs. Bobbitt, Mrs. Smith, Mrs. Brown, Mrs. Jones, Mrs. Ross, Ms. Deb Jordan, Dr. Ladner—I am humbled to have heard your stories and shared time with you. Thank you for the many contributions you have made. You are all such heroes—my heroes. I will never forget your stories, lessons, and your memories—knowing I walk in your greatness is an empowering and beautiful history. I hope I have honored your memories.

Mr. Cooper—Thank you for your expertise and for the countless hours you spent helping me curate this research—every phone call you answered, artifact you mailed, and follow-up interview you agreed to have been invaluable. I could not have done this without you, and am incredibly grateful to have you in my life.

Esteemed poets and visual artists—Claudia Rankine, Ashley M. Jones, Evie Shockley, Nate Marshall, Stanley Banks, Maxine Chernoff, Mary Ruefle, Cole Swensen, Emily Pettit, Jordan Stempleman, Michelle Taransky, Ariana Benson, Andrew Feiler, André Chung, Kevin Hopkins, Kevin Demery, Hùng Lê, Utē Petit, Rebecca Marimutu, Aliyah Bonnette, Mario Joyce, Kennedy Vincent, Good Black Art, Dolphin Archival Printing, and many others—Thank you for making the world more beautiful with art and creativity.

To my amazing tribe of friends, family, and loved ones—Thank you all for your love, laughter, friendship, and for being my chosen family.

To my blended family, Jordan and V—Our family is one of the most important aspects of my life. Thank you for loving our children and building a family centered on friendship and joy. I love and thank you forever.

Jordan—Thank you for growing up with me, for shared memories of life and our beautiful children, for igniting my love of learning and poetry, and being my forever family. I am grateful for the experiences and years we've shared.

Damian—Thank you for being my husband and best friend. Your unwavering support, your laughter, and your daily affirmations of pride and love mean so much. You are my soldier. Your love and belief in my abilities always makes me feel as if I can do anything. Your big heart and laugh are beautiful. I thank and love you endlessly.

Most importantly, to my children Bella, Townes, and Aiden—You are my entire world, my heart, and what I am most proud of in this life. I am grateful for every moment I have had the honor of witnessing your incredible lives; it has been nothing short of magical. Thank you for bringing me abounding joy. Being your mama is the most important role in my life. You are the sunshine of my life. Always.

POETIC REFLECTION

A Certain Swirl[14]
Mary Ruefle

The classroom was dark, all the desks were empty, and the sentence on the board was frightened to find itself alone. The sentence wanted someone to read it, the sentence thought it was a fine sentence, a noble, thorough sentence, perhaps a sentence of some importance, made of chalk dust, yes, but a sentence that contained within itself a certain swirl not unlike the nebulous heart of the unknown universe, but if no one read it, how could it be sure? Perhaps it was a dull sentence and that was why everyone had left the room and turned out the lights. Night came, and the moon with it. The sentence sat on the board and shone. It was beautiful to look at, but no one read it.

Mario Joyce, *Static Field*, 2023. Oil on canvas. Photo credit of artwork Mario Joyce and Sakhile&Me. "*Static Field* and *A Light Change (June Bug)* are my first experiments using soil from the farm I grew up on in the paintings." Learn more at https://mariojoyce.com.

Unlearning the Hush

CHAPTER 1

"Everybody Knows about Mississippi"

> You don't have to live next to me
> Just give me my equality
> Everybody knows about Mississippi.
> —Nina Simone, "Mississippi Goddam"

Kevin Hopkins, painting inspired by a photograph by Dorothea Lange, 2021. Oil on canvas.

POETIC REFLECTION

statistical haiku (or, how do they discount us? let me count the ways)[1]

Evie Shockley

only 3 of 100 black boys
entering kindergarten will graduate college—
in the night sky, shooting stars

every day a black person
under 20 years old commits suicide—
plucked magnolia blossom's funereal perfume

a black man is 700% more likely
than a white man to be sentenced to prison—
scattered thundershowers in may

every 3 minutes
a black child is born into poverty—
pine needles line the forest floor

after langston hughes's "johannesburg mines"

Mississippi in Historical Context

"Separate but equal" in Mississippi never existed, not even when the language came into existence with the *Plessy v. Ferguson* decision in 1896. If anything, Mississippi public schools were ground zero for a quite different mantra: structurally developed, racially separate schools were not equal in any way. What this means is that for more than half a century after *Plessy*, high-quality Black teachers in Mississippi functioned with little to no resources in buildings, facilities, gymnasiums, and classrooms that were structurally deficient, with books that were outdated or discarded hand-me-downs from all-white schools, and with few opportunities for learning (or teaching) beyond the middle grades. Mississippi in many ways mirrors the challenges we face in our country today, and so to use its history to inform how we navigate current concerns in education is important.

In 1954, *Brown v. Board of Education* legally dismantled racially segregated schools. But Mississippi public schools would not comply with *Brown* in any meaningful way until 1970. To put it another way, a child born in Mississippi at the time of the *Brown* decision would not attend a school that was in compliance with this Supreme Court ruling until they were seventeen years old or about to graduate from high school.[2] The impact of *Brown* reverberates today.

How did Black educators in Mississippi respond to the slow pace of compliance and desegregation efforts? How did they go about teaching their students how to live in a world resistant to their full inclusion or advancement? How did they find moments of joy and celebration amid the attempt to diminish Black educators and students? Education historian Jarvis Givens points out that

> Black educators have always known that their students are living in an anti-Black world and, therefore, decided that their teaching must be set against the very order of that world. Their political clarity manifested in lessons that were explicitly about race, history, and Black culture; but their views also shaped the social systems of classrooms, even at times when tenets of antiracism were not explicitly named. They took a holistic approach to teaching—honoring Black life, with all its beauty and contradictions.[3]

Despite the reality that the schools Black children in Mississippi attended were segregated by law and had resources that were inferior to those of their white counterparts prior to desegregation, it is important to remember that these Black youths had one distinct advantage: they were in the care of Black educators who affirmed Black identity and prepared students to enter a racialized and (eventually) desegregated world.[4]

"Stupidest Decision"

> The United States Supreme Court has come up with its stupidest decision—today's ruling against segregation in public school. The decision is bound to create embarrassment and distress and hinder, instead of help race relations.[5]

Dated Monday, May 18, 1954, the above quote is from a front-page editorial in a local newspaper, the *Hattiesburg American*. It illustrates the general sentiment of local decision makers in Hattiesburg as the city's paper informed residents about the U.S. Supreme Court's ruling in *Brown v. Board of Education*. This front-page editorial set the tone for the city's response to *Brown*. It is also a reminder of the efforts for over a century to keep schooling separate or nonexistent for Black people in Mississippi. This chapter contextualizes this history and outlines the long struggle of African Americans, particularly in Mississippi, to attend desegregated schools without legal restriction. It specifically focuses on the city of

Hattiesburg and the state of Mississippi, and gives a brief overview of the important role Black women played in the educational advancement of Black Mississippi communities.

"Everybody Knows about Mississippi"

To hear Nina Simone sing the words "everybody knows about Mississippi" is to hear and feel the long history her song "Mississippi Goddam" laments. There is no denying the emotions Simone's guttural singing awakens, as the lyrics and piano notes move from quiet to emphatic, her voice cracking and railing with pain. The opening lines of the song lament the racial tragedies and inequities connected to the state.[6] Mississippi is a complicated state, to say the least—socially, racially, economically, and regarding its systems of education and desegregation. Historically and to date, Mississippi continues to have some of the highest rates of poverty and socioeconomic inequality. Though the state is in many ways steeped in a history of racism and violence, it has also produced and inspired countless civically minded teachers, activists, and mentors. This includes figures such as Medgar Evers, Jeanette Smith, Peggy Jean Connor, and Ellie and Vernon Dahmer, the educators profiled in this book's chapters, and many others.[7] They would challenge the ideologies prevalent in Mississippi and leave an imprint of excellence in education that had lasting, positive social and political impact.[8]

In Mississippi, de jure and de facto segregation and Jim Crow laws were firmly in place to keep Black people aware of their social position, and violence was always a stark reality.[9] According to NAACP records, "[f]rom 1882 to 1968 there were 4,743 lynchings in the United States"; furthermore, Mississippi had "the highest number of lynchings during that time period with 581 on record.[10] These staggering statistics illustrate the severity and level of violence embedded in the state's fabric and occurring on a daily basis. In his article "Killing Emmett," Davis W. Houck includes a quote from *Black Boy*, the book that novelist Richard Wright wrote about the impact that the lynchings had on Black residents in the state:

> The penalty of death awaited me if I made a false move and I wondered if it was worthwhile to make any move at all. The things that influenced my conduct as a Negro did not have to happen to me directly; I needed but to hear of them to feel their full effects in the deepest layers of my consciousness. Indeed, the white brutality that I had not seen was a more effective control of my behavior than that which I knew.[11]

This sentiment paints an accurate picture of the racial terror present in the state. In addition to this violence, Mississippi functioned from the standpoint that Blacks were inferior and indebted to whites. Jim Crow, Black Codes, racist policies, the denial of human rights, and inequality loomed over the state. Historian Jon Hale describes this:

> Without federal supervision, legislators were free to formally write Jim Crow policy into the Constitution of 1890. Blacks were denied the right to vote, despite the constitutional guarantee decreed in the 15th Amendment. The federal government ignored this overt denial of basic human rights and dignity; African Americans were henceforth subject to policy controlled by white supremacists. The 1890 Constitution reversed the political gains and the equality promised after the Civil War. From this point forward, Jim Crow policy referred to the social customs and the formal laws that separated blacks from whites. Jim Crow would come to be the defining characteristic of life in Mississippi as numerous laws were passed that segregated blacks in public spaces.[12]

The separation and hierarchy of races, the oppression of Jim Crow laws, and the creation of policies and systems that supported the racialization of Black residents were all at the heart of historic Mississippi. These laws, policies, and characteristics influenced the overall racial climate of the state.

These aspects of the state ultimately shaped and influenced the educational system and the response to school desegregation after the *Brown* decision. Hale points out that "[t]he history of education in Mississippi is a history of segregation. The educational history of Mississippi between 1954 and 1965 illustrates how larger economic, political, and social trends intersected in such a way as to provide an inequitable education for many blacks in the state."[13] The state grappled with not only a poor educational system, but also the manipulation of educational policies that impacted Black educators, including low salaries, ever-changing certification requirements, and racially embedded hiring practices. In addition to the effects of inequitable hiring practices, segregationists and groups such as the White Citizens' Council, established in 1954, and the Mississippi State Sovereignty Commission ("a state operated spy agency"[14]), established in 1956, worked to stave off integration, ultimately helping to ensure that the state was the last to desegregate, and that Black residents felt the resistance to desegregation.[15]

The concerns about the state's education and racial sentiments permeated the Black community, especially in the period after *Brown*, as Black educators and communities knew that desegregation would likely result in worse conditions for Black educators, students, and communities, as resistance grew. Charles C. Bolton explains:

> White resistance to school desegregation proved both deep-seated and sustained, relenting only under a steady stream of legal action by black parents and federal intervention. Consequently, the elimination of Mississippi's dual educational system occurred largely on white terms. Black teachers and administrators lost their jobs and the black community saw an erosion of the control they had exercised over their children's education. In the years that followed, as federal support waned, efforts in Mississippi and across the nation to create unitary school systems usually floundered, in many cases leading to a resegregation of schools. Given the difficulties surrounding the dismantling of separate schools, it is not surprising that many have judged school integration a failure. One flaw in the process that a number of commentators have pointed to is that the attempts to achieve school integration did little to help (or even hindered) the attainment of the larger goal surrounding school integration efforts: the improvement of black education.[16]

Despite the decision in *Brown* and the passage of the Civil Rights Act, racist practices and policies ultimately shaped the landscape and conditions in which Black educators would be forced to exist, as desegregation failed to live up to its intended promises, and ultimately upended the jobs and established lives of Black educators.[17]

Mississippi is the place where Emmett Till and Medgar Evers were murdered, a state that did not have an interracial marriage until 1970, a state that banned *Sesame Street*, the site of too many instances of racial injustices and violence to name, and of the Freedom Summer murders. In contrast, it is also the home of the Mississippi Freedom Schools, the site of Woolworth sit-ins, and the place from which Fannie Lou Hamer, Myrlie Evers, Ida B. Wells, Unita Blackwell, and many others contributed greatly to the story of our country's history, ensuring that justice and equality became synonymous with the state. The dichotomy of tragic and beautiful meets here, which makes Mississippi a historically rich and worthwhile site to situate this research.

"Everybody Knows about Mississippi" 7

Map of Hattiesburg, Mississippi. http://www.mappery.com/map-of/Hattiesburg-Mississippi City-Map.

Hattiesburg, Mississippi

Hattiesburg is the fourth largest city in the state of Mississippi, with approximately forty-five thousand residents to date. The 2020 U.S. Census report reveals that Hattiesburg remains a primarily Black city, with "36% of the residents being Black and 34% of its residents at poverty level, and the median household income $36,111," further proving the historical implications that left an indelible mark on the city and state.[18] Mississippi is a state that is marked by both the historical pain of our country and the perseverance of the Black people who resided there in the 1950s through the 1970s.

Known as Hub City because of the railroads that intersected there, and founded in the 1880s by Captain Harris Hardy, who named the city after his wife Hattie, Hattiesburg was at one time a place of opportunity. However, from the 1950s to the 1970s Hattiesburg, like the entire state of Mississippi, was marked by significant violence, racism, and poverty. Hattiesburg is a bit of an anomaly. Despite being in Mississippi, its Black residents defied what was commonplace in the southern states and used the segregated ways of the city and state to build a thriving Black community. Some of the first Black residents of Hattiesburg were drawn to the city during the 1800s because of new job opportunities—"the black people who came to Hattiesburg in those early years were in some ways dropping their own mule plows and walking away from the fields of their ancestors."[19] By breaking the curse of being limited to field work, Black citizens were beginning to reimagine what life could look like despite segregation. This initial movement from what was expected of them cemented the way of thinking that the Black communities and educators in Hattiesburg would come to live by.[20] Hattiesburg became a significant place for civil rights activism and racial uplift, connected as it was to Freedom Summer, SNCC (Student Nonviolent Coordinating Committee, pronounced "snick"), voting rights advocacy, and community organizing, and home to the *many* people who actively worked to fight for justice.[21]

According to FORDETRA's records, the first Negro school system was established in 1879, and according to state records, Forrest County was the first county in Mississippi "to provide Negroes with an eight-month school term."[22] Building from this history, Hattiesburg educators and the segregated Black schools would become some of the strongest in the state. Additionally, Black educators in Hattiesburg were skilled, many with master's degrees and training in their craft.[23] Prior to desegregation, Hattiesburg schools had the most educated Black teachers in the state and higher than usual expenditures for Black students. These strong schools helped to solidify and deepen the Black community that worked to shape and enrich its students.

Hattiesburg is part of the suppressed story of what was happening in the South. But there is a counterstory: Black female educators and community members in Hattiesburg ensured the story of Hattiesburg's Black community was not dictated solely by tragedy but was interwoven with fortitude. William Sturkey reminds us that "[a]s difficult as their lives were, it is also important to remember that working-class black Hattiesburgers were a resilient and well-callused population."[24] This sense of resilience would carry through to the educators who were formative in the Black community and helped maintain a sense of pride and cohesion. Sturkey's research helps to illustrate the particular ways that Hattiesburg differed from neighboring Mississippi cities and communities—the schools, the teacher preparedness and quality, and the community were unique. Hattiesburg educators would embody not only the history of Black education, but would also provide the necessary teachings to ensure that when their students entered society they would be well equipped to actively disrupt inequities and navigate the society in which they lived.

HISTORICAL VIGNETTE
Christopher M. Span

The Importance of Mississippi History

The importance of Mississippi history cannot be overstated—it is not merely a regional narrative but a foundational component of American history itself. To understand Mississippi is to delve into the very origins of the nation, for it was founded as a slave state, and its history is intertwined with the African American experience.

The migration of Black people to Mississippi, primarily as enslaved individuals from states along the Atlantic coast, laid the groundwork for the birth of African American culture in its fullest expression. Yet, the significance of Mississippi extends beyond its borders, as the outmigration of African Americans to other regions carried with it the rich tapestry of their hopes, dreams, and cultural values.

While Mississippi may be synonymous with slavery and cotton, it is essential to recognize that Black people did not merely endure these hardships—they carried with them the seeds of resilience, determination, and cultural richness wherever they went. This diaspora of African American culture, manifested in the establishment of schools, the evolution of music from sorrow songs to the blues, and everyday acts of extraordinary perseverance, serves as a testament to the indomitable spirit of the African American community.

My research, for instance, explores how African American cultural values shaped the development of public education and influenced the evolution of music genres. Mississippi's impact on the nation's cultural landscape cannot be overstated—it is a crucible where the African American experience is both defined by pain and redefined by resilience, joy, and empowerment.

Indeed, the African American experience embodies a unique narrative of sacrifice and triumph, epitomizing the enduring spirit of a people who have overcome immense challenges to carve out their place in the world. In understanding Mississippi history, we gain insight into the complexities of the American story and honor the remarkable contributions of African Americans to the fabric of our nation.

Kevin Demery, *Burning Bridges*, 2023. Pinewood, MDF, acrylic, shackle and chain, and handheld chalkboard. 2.5ft height × variable dimensions. "This sculpture references civil rights icon Ruby Bridges and their activism as a child by being the first African American to attend a formerly whites-only public school. As America reflects on its educational past, it is essential to see that gains in antidiscrimination laws in education have not fully protected Black communities from their very histories being erased."

POETIC REFLECTION

Love Poem in the Black Field[25]
Ariana Benson

Caroline County, Virginia, 1954
for Mildred and Richard

The darkness we need is possible only in myth.
    We, like the titans, are almost certainly too much;
Us laid flat on my quilt, this antebellum tapestry
    Beneath our backs, our heaving ribs pressing valleys
Into the June bugs' grass. And it is theirs, this grass,
    Because it was theirs first. I'm afraid, more than you
Can fathom, that we will die if we touch. If we so much as
    Look. So do what you can with the glancing, gaze trained,
Instead, on the stars under whom we bask; tranquil, without fear
    Of joining them in their hanging. Many pasts have made me
Their captive. I was theirs first, long before I was mine.
    For now, we wait out the setting: the red, the orange,
The melting heavens. Anticipate that precious absence
    Of light. I tell you *a vivid sunset means the world*
Below is one day closer to dead, and you know I mean *beauty*
    Is never just that; is not to be trusted. I trust myself, somehow,
Less. I wish this thing I hold for you was plain, expected.
    A pale blue vein cradled nightly in a warm, black grasp.
You say *the moon gives off no glow of its own, merely reflecting*
    What the sun has to spare. And I understand our love
Is nothing without that sun under whose glare it will surely
    burn. *Yes*, I say, *how beautiful*; and we would be.
How beautifully close to dead.

CHAPTER 2

The Wisdom of Elders

I need to know their names
those women I would have walked
with . . .
—Lucille Clifton, *The Lost Women*

Hùng Lê, *I Wish the Rain Had Come That Day*, 2023. This piece was made using laser engraving on indigo fabric and then adding embroidery. The image is of the artist hugging his grandmother before he left Vietnam. There is a yearning that the rain will come and delay the flight, so there will be more time left to be with family. "This art relates to oral history because objects hold meaning and are imbued with the maker's hands, intentions, and wishes. I wanted to make an object that would carry the story of my grandmother into the future." Learn more at https://hunglestudio.com.

POETIC REFLECTION

Cartography

Emily Pettit[1]

This is a jar of us and it gives.
Other things are meant to float by.
It's an ocean over there.
Hear it. Here we are standing.
You have always been with me.
That's just how my hear works.
Hands are for holding. This is my
hand. How you have it. How you are
holding it. Holding this heart.
This love makes the sun feel
that close to you. Being the breeze part
of the breeze it's with ease you bend
to this. When your voice is a vision.
I have of home.

The Journey to This History

One evening my momma shared a story about Mrs. Jemye Heath. Mrs. Heath had been her sixth grade teacher, whom she had remained in touch with all these years later. She reminisced about Mrs. Heath's lasting impression on her life and retold stories I'd heard many times before. I asked if anyone had ever recorded Mrs. Heath's story or honored her dedication to students and community, and Momma laughed and responded that no one would likely care about the story of a Hattiesburg teacher. However, at that moment, I knew that her story and others needed to be documented.

I wondered how their stories might fill in questions I had about my own experiences as an educator and offer guidance for navigating current concerns in education. I also wondered what these women's experiences might tell us about the impact of the diminished representation of Black educators in education systems after *Brown v. Board of Education*. What can we learn from their stories to inform our understanding of collective work and pedagogy in classrooms today?

Charles Payne reminds us that "[w]e do not ordinarily realize how much the well-publicized activism of the sixties depended upon the efforts of older activists who worked in obscurity throughout the 1940s and 1950s."[2] The same remains true today, as education present day should encompass the perspectives and expertise of historical educators. Their histories can guide how we approach education today, allowing current educators to be more aptly informed and offering us space to consider the gaps in our knowledge of the histories of others. I cannot think of a more pertinent time in our history to make certain that these voices are amplified and that these stories are documented for future educators and generations.

The Knowing of Names

The lines of Lucille Clifton's poem *the lost women* resonate. She asks, "Where are my mislaid sisters? All the women who could have known me, where in the world are their names?"

The idea that women, Black women in particular, are nameless or lost is a sentiment that should give us pause. These women are not nameless, and they need to be included in the historical record. Their very stories affirm our existence, our contributions, our reasons for reaching back into the past to reclaim and retell what has always been here. It is not by coincidence that so many of the leaders of movements for social justice emerged from Hattiesburg, Mississippi, and so in the following pages their faces will become visible and their stories known. Black women have always been full of greatness.

The stories of this book's participants remind me of what Alex Haley, the author of *Roots*, once wrote about the importance of storytelling, memory, and the value of speaking with your elders: "And every evening, after the supper dishes were washed, they would go out on the front porch and sit in cane-bottomed rocking chairs, and I would always sit behind grandma's chair. And every single evening of those summers, unless there was some particularly hot gossip that would overrule it, they would talk about the same thing. It was bits and pieces and patches of what I later would learn was a long narrative history of the family which had been passed down across generations."[3]

Smithsonian Secretary Lonnie Bunch continues this notion:

> I believe that tension is the way to understand the American experience. So, part of the notion is that what memory is, is the life through the eyes

of a particular individual, a particular community, or a particular family. Memory is so powerful and so right.[4]

Understanding the importance of these personal accounts and memories is essential to our understanding of history at large. In *The Oral History Reader*, Alessandro Portelli reflects, "Oral sources tell us not just what people did, but what they wanted to do, what they believed they were doing."[5] And Paul Thompson continues:

> Nevertheless, oral history certainly can be a means for transforming both the content and the purpose of history. It can be used to change the focus of history itself, and open up new areas of inquiry; it can break down barriers between teachers and students, between generations, between educational institutions and the world outside; and in the writing of history—whether in books, or museums, or radio and film—it can give back to the people who made and experienced history through their own words, a central place.[6]

The journeys of participants represent a broader look at what Black female educators endured and accomplished throughout history. Following the table below is a brief narrative and overview of the contributors in this chapter. Those interviewed are referred to as both participants and contributors, as participant does not adequately capture the importance of their expert role regarding this research. The oral histories begin with Secretary Lonnie Bunch, as his knowledge of history helped establish the foundation as I began my research. The oral histories following Secretary Bunch's are ordered from youngest participant to eldest, to symbolize that we stand on the shoulders of the greats who came before us, building on their legacies and efforts. The interviews are in the participants' own words, with slight modifications for grammar and clarity, as I felt it was important to honor what the participants said and keep the original content intact.

TABLE 1. Contributors and Participants

Contributor's Name	Position	Years Teaching
Armstrong, Linda	Student and Daughter of a Hattiesburg Teacher	N/A
Bobbitt, Mary	Educator	30 years
Bunch, Lonnie	Historian, Educator, Secretary of the Smithsonian	N/A
Brown, Julia	Student	N/A
Cooper, Charles	Student and Educator	27 years
Dahmer, Bettie	Student and Daughter of Activists Vernon and Ellie Dahmer	N/A
Dahmer, Ellie	Educator and Activist	38 years
Davis, Trinity	President of Teachers Like Me and Educator	N/A
Fowler, Katherine	Educator	44 years
Funchess, Glenda	Student and Civil Rights Lawyer	N/A
Goins, Dolores	Educator	31 years
Hale-Green, Carolyn	School Counselor	35 years
Heath, Jemye	Educator and Principal	43 years
Harris, Anthony	Student and Educator	47 years
Jones, Barbara Elaine	Educator	37 years
Ladner, Joyce	Student, Educator, Activist	22 years
Manning, Alva	Educator	20 years
Woullard, Rosetta	Educator and Principal	37 years
Ross, Barbara	Educator	26 years
Smith, Freddye	Educator	23 years
FORDETRA Hattiesburg Members	Hattiesburg Residents, Community Members, Former Educators, and Students (100+ Members)	N/A

CHAPTER 2

Oral History of Secretary Lonnie Bunch
*Secretary of Smithsonian Institution,
Historian, Educator*

Secretary Lonnie Bunch is a trailblazer and by strange chance, he is also my husband's cousin, so by marriage and proxy I can proudly claim him as part of my family. It was an honor to speak with such a great historian and human being. His insights added depth to the historical aspects of my research. During the interview I asked him how he would approach telling this story if he were telling it, and why understanding the stories that took place during desegregation is so important, and his response is below. Though he's not from Mississippi, Secretary Bunch's vast expertise about that time period offered important historical context. His knowledge of general history, Black history, and our country's history, and his understanding of the importance of stories made his interview an ideal way to deepen the stories I collected. His bio on the Smithsonian website reads:

> Lonnie G. Bunch III is the 14th Secretary of the Smithsonian. As Secretary, he oversees 19 museums, 21 libraries, the National Zoo, numerous research centers, and several education units and centers.

Secretary Lonnie Bunch. Photo courtesy of the Smithsonian Institution.

Previously, Bunch was the director of the Smithsonian's National Museum of African American History and Culture. When he started as director in July 2005, he had one staff member, no collections, no funding and no site for a museum. Driven by optimism, determination and a commitment to build "a place that would make America better," Bunch transformed a vision into a bold reality.[7]

Secretary Bunch's work as a historian is deeply connected to community, as he discusses in an interview with the *Washington Post*: "I want to talk to the elders within the African American community. I want to get their sense, and their blessing, and an artifact or two," Bunch says. He wants to pin down the stories about the beginnings of desegregation. "I've begun to think about the transformative generation, the link between the bad times and good times," he says.[8] This interview and his approach to history inspired the art exhibit I cocurated at the Haw Contemporary Gallery in Kansas City to illuminate the oral histories in this book.

"First of all, it is impossible for a nation to move forward unless it understands its past and understands, not in a negative way, but in a way that says, here is the candid truth about our experiences, but here is how that struggle has made some important changes. In essence, what you want is for people to realize that the strength of this country is people who challenge it to live up to its stated ideals. In a way, what many people who fought against desegregation really believed is they were aspirational. They believed in what the country says it is, not what it is. So, that's important, I think, for people to understand. It's a story that's rich with real information about policy, prejudice, politics, but also about how individuals crossed racial and political lines to effect change."

When asked about some of the hurdles that Black female teachers face, Lonnie shared: "Black teachers' credentials are questioned and undermined. They are seen as not as good as the other teachers. They are seen as though their place is just with Black students, can they teach white students. . . . There are a variety of fundamental important questions that really get at the structures that both supported and limited Black education."[9]

When asked how he would approach telling these stories, Secretary Bunch answered, "I think that it is this real tension between tragedy and resilience despair and hope, right? That's the way to understand the Black community. I think that what you've come across by having these oral histories, and what you realize, is that the great strength of Black America is their ability to imagine a world anew. That is really the great strength. The thing that always amazes me: in the heart of being in a segregated world, how did people who only had that experience, how did they imagine a better world? For their kids, grandkids, maybe even for themselves. That's the great strength, I think, of Black community. So, that's why I think your research is important. I would argue that the way to tell the story is through the individual hopes and aspirations, but it's also really a way to say that you owe all those people who fought that fight. You need, whoever 'you' is, to be an activist, at least, in doing the best you can to help a country live up to its ideals. Your task is to make sure that those memories, those words don't get lost.

"I believe that tension is the way to understand the American experience. So, part of the notion is that what memory is, is life through the eyes of a particular individual, a particular community, or a particular family. Memory is so powerful and so right. There are other times where that memory is full of misstatements, and it's not as accurate. History is this sort of bulwark of accuracy. History, sometimes, the way it's written can be bloodless. Sometimes it loses the passion. So, for me, I think historians are better when they are shaped by the living community. That's what oral history and memory does. It allows a living community to shape its past in profound ways. And so that's what I mean. That's why the tension means that a little bit of both makes for a much better history.

"The price of liberty, the price of freedom is eternal struggle. The notion that somehow you make it to the promise land, rather than seeing the promise land, I would argue that what you see are changes. Whether it is desegregation, etc., these are steps, but they are not the promise land, they are steps to it. . . . The other thing that you said that is really important to recognize is that there is a profound need for Black spaces. It's profound on several levels. On one hand, one of the challenges of desegregation was that you move away from Black spaces, right? That sort of integration became the promise land. So, rather than go to Joe's store that you've gone to for twenty years, you go to the Giant or wherever it is, because you can now do it. So, I think that what we really need to recognize is that without those spaces, you lose the opportunity to be yourself. You lose the opportunity to be shaped by a community. You lose the opportunity of saying, 'I need help and this space helped me do what I need to do.' That's why it's important for me to build museums. It's important to also create conceptual spaces, whether it's through oral histories, or whatever so that you have an opportunity—there always is a Black reservoir to dip into."[10] My time with Secretary Bunch reinforced the importance of ancestry, stories, and the role that history plays in all of it.

Oral History of Ms. Bettie Dahmer
*Student at Forrest County Public Schools
and Daughter of Educator/Activist*

I had the honor of meeting Ms. Bettie Dahmer through Dr. Joyce Ladner. Bettie Dahmer is a wealth of knowledge. She is the daughter of Mrs. Ellie Dahmer (educator and activist) and the late Mr. Vernon Dahmer (activist) and was a student in Forrest County Public Schools. Her story illustrates the strength, intergenerational connectedness, and legacy of our stories.

"I attended Mattie Robinson Kindergarten until May of 1961. I also attended Earl Travillion from September of 1961 until December of 1970. In January of 1971, I was at North Forrest High School, and I graduated from North Forrest in May of 1972 with honors. I did not know that I was graduating with honors until I saw it printed on the program that night. I did not get the gold cord that honors students receive because I had refused to join the Beta Club. When I first arrived at North Forrest,

Ms. Bettie Dahmer, student at Forrest County Schools.

90 percent of the students were not in attendance because white parents did not want their children going to school with Black students. White parents and students boycotted, and white parents were outside protesting saying, 'niggers go home.' I had a Caucasian teacher who would refuse to say Negro, he said Nigra (the closest he could get to saying Nigger without saying it). The students staged a walkout because of this. The principal said he would expel us all and place it in our permanent records if the students staged another walkout. I told the principal that if he did, I would make the media aware of the expulsions and the reasons why. Suddenly the teacher learned how to say Negro correctly, and no one was expelled. As a student I was always told that my academic efforts had to be three times better to be considered equal.

"Black female educators served as mothers, counselors, and mentors to their pupils. I would rate 80 percent as adequate or above. My mother, Mrs. Ellie Dahmer, was an educator and was not in the classroom from June to August of each year. One of her favorite quotes was 'idle hands are the devil's workshop.' I was raised on a farm and performed manual labor in the Mississippi heat. At ten years old, I could drive a tractor and shoot a shotgun. As a career, I wanted an indoor job with air conditioning, so I worked as a government employee.

"I believe that Black women lift up the youth and serve as visual examples of the progress that is possible. The civil rights movement would not have been successful without Black women in education.

"Although *Brown versus Board* was federal law in 1954, actual desegregation in Forrest County, Mississippi did not occur until January of 1971. Private academies were opened to maintain racial segregation. In north Mississippi, Black business owners paid a tax that supported the white academies, and it was collected by the white sheriff. In order to have a Black business, you paid money to the white academies to help them operate. There are thirty-two schools in Mississippi that are currently as of January 12, 2024, under federal desegregation order.

"After desegregation, one hundred thousand Black educators were purged and replaced by less qualified people. I believe the prison pipeline was one of the outcomes of integration. In Mississippi, progress is still being fought for on a daily basis—for example, state attorney Lynn Fitch's attempt to use federal Covid funds to fund predominantly white private schools and academies, and thwart the implementation of the *Ayers* decision [*Ayers v. Fordice*]. Mississippi is better than it used to be.

"I would encourage future educators to be an example for others, use curriculum that matters, and teach students about Ida B. Wells, Emmett Till, Vernon Dahmer, and others who worked to make a difference."[11]

Oral History of Dr. Anthony Harris
Student at Hattiesburg Public Schools and Educator, 47 Years

Dr. Anthony Harris was a student in Hattiesburg Public Schools and would later become an educator. His bio gives us this information:

> Mr. Harris was born in Hattiesburg, Mississippi in 1953. During his preteen and teen years, he was an active participant in the local Civil Rights Movement. After graduating from high school in 1971, he attended the University of Southern Mississippi where he earned a bachelor's degree in Spanish in 1974 and a master's degree in counseling in 1976. In 1979, he moved to Commerce, Texas to pursue a doctorate in Counseling at East Texas State University (now Texas A&M University—Commerce). After completing his doctorate degree in 1982, he remained at Texas A&M University—Commerce for 17 years, serving in a variety of positions, including Director of the Counseling Center, Associate Professor, Assistant to the President, and Associate Vice President for Resource Development. As a leader in the City of Commerce, he served for 15 years as a member of the Board of Trustees of the Commerce Independent

Dr. Anthony Harris, student at Forrest County Schools and educator.

School District. In 1988, the W. K. Kellogg Foundation selected him to participate in the 9th Class of the Kellogg National Fellowship Program, which allowed him to hone his leadership skills and to visit 17 countries, primarily in developing and Third World countries.

Dr. Harris cares deeply about advocacy and has continued his lifelong commitment to advancing justice and education.

"I would describe my education in Mississippi as the best it could have been, given the Jim Crow laws and segregated schools. My elementary education and one year of junior high occurred at all-Black schools. My Black teachers worked in a system that was intentionally designed to provide an inferior education to Black children. In every grade, teachers and students were given used and outdated textbooks that the white schools had discarded for updated versions. The intent was to make sure that white children reaped the benefits of updated new information and knowledge and Black students would not. Despite those efforts from white administrators, our Black teachers taught from the heart, not from the textbook. They were the best teachers I ever had because they refused to be complicit in efforts to treat Black children as being unworthy of a good education. They raised expectations and insisted that we reach or exceed those high expectations. In 1966, going into the eighth grade, I was part of a group of five Black students who desegregated an all-white junior high school. It was at Thames Junior High that I encountered unforeseen acts of racism from classmates and diminished expectations from white teachers.

"I attended Mary Bethune Elementary School (grades 1–6, all-Black); Lillie Burney Junior High School (7th grade, all-Black); Thames Junior High School (grades 8–9, white); Blair High School (grades 10–11, white); Rowan High School (12th grade, all-Black). Two memorable experiences among so many stand out. When I was in second grade, Mrs. McGown assigned homework in our workbooks for the following day. I somehow managed to spill red Kool-Aid on my workbook and was unable to complete the assignment. The next day, Mrs. McGown asked why I hadn't completed the assignment. I knew it would do no good to tell her what happened. She used a black fanbelt and whacked me three times on my back. After I became an adult, I visited Mrs. McGown and told her about the incident. She didn't remember it and apologized profusely to me. I told her that I was not seeking an apology. Instead, I wanted to say thanks. At the time of the whacks, I thought she was just a mean woman. But as an adult, I know what she and my other Black teachers were trying to do. They wanted us to excel to the point where we would not be just as good as our white counterparts. We would have to be twice as smart. I told her that her message warned us to avoid doing just enough to get by, accepting mediocrity, and thinking that we are not as smart as white kids.

"The other experience was at Thames Junior High, where I was called the N-word every day and had to resist the temptation to retaliate when a white classmate spat on me. On another occasion, the day after Dr. King was assassinated, my white classmates wildly and openly celebrated with laughter and jokes, all in my presence. I found myself in the lion's den every single day. But I was not going to let their bigotry and acts of violence keep me from being distracted. Instead, I started internalizing the messages from my elementary Black teachers about perseverance and believing in myself.

"My Black female teachers provided the appropriate balance between challenge and support. For example, if we were having trouble with a math problem, they would help us until we figured it out. But if we refused to listen or didn't take their help seriously, the black fanbelt came out. Moreover, they had grown up and lived in Jim Crow South, which drove their efforts less toward protecting us from racism and bigotry and more toward preparing us for how to handle acts of racism and bigotry. For me, that came in handy when I was confronted daily with racial slurs and physical attacks from white students at Thames Junior High School.

"My experience as a Black student in the Hattiesburg separate school system probably was influential in my decisions in my career decisions. Being raised and educated in Hattiesburg by loving parents and dedicated teachers, I learned and internalized values such as compassion, fairness, justice, courage, selflessness, etc. I believe those values aided me in becoming a therapist and a committed advocate for racial and social justice.

"My own learning experiences have definitely been shaped by race. It is not a matter of whether. It's a matter of to what extent. Being raised in segregated Hattiesburg, I was reminded daily of the presence of Jim Crow, such as separate water fountains, separate libraries, riding on the back of the bus, separate birth and death announcements in the newspaper by race, separate trash pickup days, separate schools, separate swimming pools, separate restaurant entrances, separate seating at the movie theater, etc. I learned from my mother that remaining silent and compliant was not acceptable. Wherever injustice and racism exist, one must be prepared to act. For example, in my career as a faculty member at a predominately white institution (PWI) in Texas, I worked in a department that resisted efforts to create a culture of inclusion. At the time, there were five Black faculty members. When I left after five years, there were none. I organized the Black faculty to form a resistance to the efforts of white faculty to rid the department of Black faculty members."[12]

Oral History of Mrs. Julia Brown
Student at Forrest County Public Schools and Counselor (LPC), 34 Years

I met Mrs. Julia Brown through her involvement with FORDETRA (Forrest County/DePriest/Travillion), which is a school reunion group that formed in 1990 and now consists of approximately a hundred people. The group works to preserve historical information and maintain a sense of connection to former classmates. Mrs. Brown shared photos with me of former teachers and agreed to share her experiences as a student in Forrest County Public Schools.

"My education in the state of Mississippi was stellar based on the subpar resources such as used books and very limited or no educational materials. I encountered very good teachers at Earl Travillion. Many of them

Mrs. Julia Brown, student at Forrest County Schools and counselor.

had master's degrees from large universities outside the state. They were extremely professional and exposed us to the arts and other extracurricular activities. They expected us to succeed.

"I attended Earl Travillion Attendance Center. Some of my most memorable experiences were participating in the state spelling bee. I also had a teacher who exposed us to the arts by teaching us to dance to Tchaikovsky's 'Waltz of the Flowers.' I also had memorable experiences in the choir and band. Black female teachers were often an extension of our homes. Many of my teachers knew my mother personally. My father died when I was in second grade and my teacher made me an outfit to wear to the funeral. Our teachers came to our home, prepared food as well as cleaned, and some even came to our churches.

"My own education was spread around somewhat. I went to Earl Travillion for eleven and a half years and finished the last semester of my senior year at Petal High School due to forced desegregation. I went to Tougaloo College for two years. Then I got married and started back to college after few years at Troy State University on Maxwell Air Force Base, as my then husband was in the Air Force and stationed at that base. I completed two more semesters there. I finally finished my BA in Psychology at Mississippi College in Clinton, Mississippi. I went on to get my master's in counseling psychology at the University of Southern Mississippi. So, I came full circle back home. I think in my heart I wanted to be a helper of people, but I just did not want to teach. I eventually ended up as a counselor/therapist serving adolescents in a middle school for several years. I am certain that I was influenced to become a therapist by all the various people that came across my life path. I have no regrets. I am still doing online therapy as a counselor today.

"Race has always been very prevalent in my life and my education. At Tougaloo College, I was able to really embrace my ethnicity. We wore our hair natural and saw the beauty of dressing in African attire, such as dashikis and caftans. I experienced prejudice and exclusion at Mississippi College. I experienced race in hiring practices when I worked at Pine Belt mental health care in being passed over for jobs, and saw it happen to others as well. We all persevered!

"Black women have been referred to as the 'mules of the world.' We keep pushing, we don't give up and we don't allow anyone else that we are with to quit or give up just because something is hard. We always rise just like in Maya Angelou's famous poem and Yolanda Adam's song.

"After integration, all-Black schools were downgraded from being attendance centers serving first through twelfth grade to only sixth grade or eighth grade. Black teachers who had master's degrees who taught on the high school level were assigned to middle school and junior high. High-achieving Black students were disenfranchised and lost their status at the top percentile of their classes when we were sent to the white schools. I was one of them. We still carry the emotional trauma of those times. I have classmates who still become tearful when we talk about it and remember.

"I wish we could have remained in our own schools and had them upgraded to receive the same resources that the white schools had instead of getting used books and not having essentials that we needed. We were never accepted and to this very day we are still not accepted or valued by our white counterparts."[13]

Oral History of Mr. Charles Cooper
*Student at Forrest County Public
Schools and Educator, 24 years*

Including the students of the women in this study was important to better understand the overall, direct impact their teaching had on students,

Mr. Charles Cooper, student at Forrest County Schools and educator.

including male students. Mr. Charles Cooper was a student in Forrest County Public Schools and would go on to become a teacher himself. Mr. Cooper was born and raised in Hattiesburg. He attended DePriest High School and later Earl Travillion High School, where he graduated in 1964. He later attended William Carey College, where he double majored in social science and elementary education. His teachers included Mrs. Heath, Mrs. Fowler, Mr. Fowler, and others. He had dreams of becoming a lawyer but knew his parents could not afford law school. He chose the path of teaching for his career. He taught elementary education for four years after graduating college. Mr. Cooper taught for twenty years at Gulf Coast Community College before retiring. He also was the first official golf coach at the college and was later inducted into the college's hall of fame. Mr. Cooper has a master's in administration. Although he is now retired, he remains active in the community. He is open in sharing how valuable his education was and hails the educators he had while growing up as incredible teachers and mentors.

"Attending segregated schools was one of the best parts of growing up. There were some differences that existed between the Black and white schools, of course—used books from the white schools in the county was the biggest difference. We would receive books with five or six names in the cover, and we knew that meant that the books were at least six years old, as each name represented a year that white schools used it. Schools were segregated and there were no interactions between schools, and students at that time accepted the hand-me-downs we received.

"My high school had mostly male teachers. In elementary and junior high, most of my teachers were female. I think they were role models. In my day we had no counselors or advisors. If you were Black and you were in a Black school in the 1960s, you had choices of preaching, teaching, secretarial work, or nursing. You either teach or preach, was the saying. Out of forty-six students who graduated with me from Earl Travillion High School, twenty-six students went to college. Of those twenty-six, twenty-five majored in education. So many people from the community wanted to become teachers. It was a respected profession. Despite the fact that professions were limited for Blacks, the teaching profession was one that the Black students entered into because they wanted to help create positive change. Deep down, I wanted to be an attorney, but I knew my parents could never afford to send me to law school, so I decided to teach.

"Black female teachers served as role models and advisors for students. My role models were Mr. and Mrs. Fowler. They were both teachers who impacted the lives of so many students. The teachers cared, showed concern, and I felt like they cared for me as an individual. I don't think children today have that in schools. Our schools lacked resources, but our teachers knew about teaching. In 1957 DePriest had no gym. We played basketball with goals in the dirt. Our books were used. There is nothing more hurtful than receiving a used book with numerous names in it. . . . All that is left of DePriest is the cafeteria. No one knows where the artifacts from these schools went. I tried at one point to create an archive at the cafeteria that is left. Eureka (a former school, now a museum) is beautiful—they went in there and gutted it and made it beautiful. It's a museum. Our history should have been preserved. The five county schools (DePriest, Bay Springs, Springfield, John White, and Myers) were all consolidated into one, which became Earl Travillion in 1957. The DePriest cafeteria is the only facility that is standing today, and it is a shame that all of that history is gone. I wish young people knew these stories.

"I always say that I wish that my children had the opportunities that I had in a segregated school versus what they have in an integrated school. In the segregated school, I could be class president, the best math student, etc. When students went to integrated schools, we lost that opportunity. There are so many success stories that came out of Hattiesburg because of this—for example, people like Vermester Jackson, who attended William Carey College.

"All of our parents in the community wanted the children to have a better life—one filled with success and opportunities. That was the role of all grandparents and parents in the community. They wanted us to go to college, get a degree, and be better than what they had been. All of the community people worked to make sure this happened. When I went to Zola Jackson's house, she was my mother. Everyone looked out for everyone's child. We were segregated, but we had it made. We all looked out for everyone in the community. We loved our childhoods and upbringing. There were very few selfish individuals—everyone shared what they had. If you were hungry and your neighbor had a cake, he or she would cut that cake in half and share.

"The Forrest County Negro schools were established in 1879. In 1919 an eight-month school year term was established. In 1957 all schools became Earl Travillion Attendance Center. In 1957 schools were combined and consolidated. They did this to save money and closed the other schools (the Black schools). Travillion was state of the art, but it was all about maintaining the look of separate but equal. It was originally a Black high school that encompassed all the Black high schools, then it became a junior high school after integration, and then an elementary school. Today it is currently a junior high, and the majority of teachers are white. Before the consolidation, DePriest was a large school that encompassed Palmers

Crossing and the sixteenth section neighborhood. It included several schools: John White is in Brooklyn, Mississippi and is about twenty-five miles from Hattiesburg. Myers was a county school, Springfield was about fifteen to twenty miles from Hattiesburg, and Royal Street (later named Rowan) was a neighborhood school that was within walking distance, and so forth. When the schools were closed, most of what was inside of them was gone too. . . . Yearbooks were called annuals, but the only one I have is from 1962. So much of that history is just gone.

"I could walk to William Carey College but could not attend it because of segregation. In order to go to college, I had to ride the Greyhound bus for four or five hours to attend Coahoma Junior College in Clarksdale. When William Carey finally integrated, I was the first upperclassman (junior) to enroll—I transferred there in 1966. I finished college there and graduated from William Carey in 1967. The school was white, and there were only two Blacks in 1965, so it was rough. I double majored in social science and elementary education. I taught elementary education for four years. There was one of my young white students (Don) who kept going home to his father talking about me. His father called me and asked me to meet him, so in May of 1974, I went and met with the father. We talked extensively, and toward the end of our conversation, he asked me if I had a master's degree. He said, 'Let me talk to my dean at where I teach, and maybe we can offer you a job.' Two weeks later, he offered me a job at the community college, and I accepted it. He invited me to play golf, and I became the first official coach for golf at the community college, and was later inducted into the hall of fame at the Gulf Coast Community College. I have my master's in administration. I loved teaching. I enjoyed working with elementary students and the college students. I taught at the community college for twenty years and later inducted Kenny Hughes into the golf hall of fame. I was later a pallbearer at Dean Ed Scarborough's funeral. That story shows you that when you get to know people, race doesn't matter. I've always said that as a teacher, I want to be remembered as someone who cared about all students. Like the old Negro spiritual: 'May the Work I've Done Speak for Me.' Give me opportunities, and I will succeed. Just look at me as a man. Don't categorize me beyond that. If we could just do that, we could make some progress. We all look the same in the dark. Let's do what's best for institutions and students so that everyone can reap the benefits.

"We don't have Black teachers in Mississippi because the standardized tests are so stringent. We need to teach teachers HOW to teach, not how to pass a test. We need to up the salary. It's $35,000 in Mississippi. States across the country should have the same pay and the same classes.

"I want the future teachers and generations to know the history of Black schools, the history of going to school at predominantly Black schools, the history of where Black teachers were educated (Jackson State and Alcorn). Let our history be known because it is not known. The Black and Brown students now (especially at the white schools) do not know what they are capable of. Earl Travillion, formerly a Black school, still has a 95 percent Black student body, with primarily white teachers. That is an example of how integration impacted schools and erased history. These students would shine like new money if they attended schools with students like them. Learn the history."[14]

• • •

Dear Future Generations,

Sixty years ago, as students at Earl Travillion High School in Hattiesburg, Mississippi, we were fighting for the same things that Black Americans are fighting for today. When will we ever achieve equal rights in this country? My prayer is that you all will live in a country where you will only be judged by your character and not your skin color. There are times when I wished the world could be totally dark, with no light; therefore we would all be the same color. Oh, how I dream of the day when you will no longer face discrimination.

Oh, how I wish you, my children, and other children could have had the experience of attending an all-Black school in Mississippi in the sixties. Your opportunity to be a class officer, valedictorian, salutatorian, an honor student, and many other positions would have been much easier to achieve. I still remember the proms, dances, football and basketball games, class trips, eating soul food in the cafeteria, and many other activities too numerous to name. Also, every employee, whether a janitor, secretary, bus driver, teacher, principal, cook in the cafeteria, and coach, all were advisors, counselors, and mentors for each of us. A time gone too soon and how I wished you all could have experienced it.

I can truthfully say that we have work to do, and we are not there yet to reach equality. I can still hear the prayers of my forefathers and mothers wanting us to be free. Everyone in this country needs to take a good look at themselves and make sure we are doing everything we can to make this country better. We should have a goal to be a country of, by, and for the people. God, I beseech you to allow this to happen during their lifetime.

Sincerely,
Charles Cooper

Oral History of Mrs. Barbara Elaine Jones
Educator, 37 years

Mrs. Barbara Elaine Jones was an educator in Hattiesburg Public Schools for thirty-seven years. She is certified in K–12 education, with a minor in math. After retirement, she tutored as a volunteer at her old high school for eight years to give back to the community. She remains dedicated to education, advocates for voting rights, and helps the community.

"In 1964 I graduated from Earl Travillion High School. I started junior college in the Delta, and after that I went to William Carey College in 1967. I received my BS in education K–12, with a minor in math. I started working on my master's but decided to focus on my family instead. I got married in December 1968, and later had my son and daughter. I started teaching in 1969, two years before desegregation. I had my son and was doing my student teaching at Mary Bethune (a Black school). I worked with a Black teacher (Mrs. Katherine Fowler) who I was happy to learn from,

Mrs. Barbara Elaine Jones, educator.

and she took me under her wing. Soon after starting my student teaching, I received a call from the principal from a school called W.H. Jones. He asked me if I was interested in a teaching position at the school. He asked me to leave Bethune and go to W.H. Jones (all-Black school) to finish my student teaching and start a position because another teacher was going on maternity leave. I made $9,000 for my first full year of teaching in 1969.

"I taught at several different schools in Hattiesburg. After W.H. Jones, I taught at Warsaw Elementary School, an integrated school. Mr. Ellis Kelly was the principal, and I had a blend of both second and third grade, and then taught some fourth grade after that. The students were very different from the students at W.H. Jones. At W.H. Jones and Warsaw I taught every subject—reading, science, math, music, PE, all the subjects. Teachers did not get a break during the day—we taught straight through. The schools did not even have a librarian. I was moved from W.H. Jones to Thames, and almost cried when I was told I had to move there. The teachers said that the white families gave the Black teachers a hard time, but I really enjoyed my time there. I worked there for eight years, and then I went back to W.H. Jones. Hattiesburg schools did some redistricting after integration in 1971 and 1972. This disrupted where children attended school, because it meant students had to move to a school that they had not attended most of their lives. I retired from Hawkins (it was a junior high, but it was later turned into an elementary school).

"Integration brought about many changes. In some ways it was good, and in others it was not. Nowadays, teachers do not have good relationships with students. The white teachers seem afraid of the Black students. I am still in Mississippi's NEA (National Education Association) and MAE (Mississippi Association of Educators). When I tutored at Travillion after I retired, I made sure I was a part of the NEA. I retired in December 2005 to help take care of my mother, who was bedridden. She passed in 2006, so I am grateful that I took that time with her.

"I had wonderful teachers growing up. Mrs. Heath was my teacher in fourth grade when I attended school as a child, and then we taught together at Jones Elementary. Mr. Fowler was also my teacher. Mrs. Fowler was my supervising teacher when I did my student teaching. The teachers I had growing up were so devoted. I wanted to be just like Mrs. Heath and Mrs. Fowler when I grew up. They were my role models. I looked up to them. They dressed up and looked so professional every single day at school. They were smart and expected us to do well. When I was a teacher, I tried to do things they had done. On Fridays, for example, we would talk about current events and history. I always did things to make sure that my students were ahead academically. I would buy the *Highlights* magazines and books for my classes. We worked on spelling and word searches to practice. I tried to make learning fun. I worked to explain things step by step so that students understood the material well. I had a student who I taught math to, who said he learned more from me during summer school than he did the whole year before. I loved my kids. I hugged them each morning and told them how important they were. I made students aware that I cared about them and wanted them to learn as if they were my own children.

"Some of the benefits of integration were that our Black students no longer got torn books and no resources. Black kids got new books like the white kids. Integration was a problem because of the redistricting that occurred. When the white schools would throw books out, I would save those books and give them to my students.

"When I first started teaching, all school supplies came out of the teacher's pocket; there was no money from the state department, and so either the teachers bought their own, or they had to do without supplies. Years later, in the 1980s, teachers were allotted $200 for the year for supplies. I was always told by principals that my students were well prepared for the next grade. Some of the downsides to integration was that it was forced. The school system was better when there was discipline in the school and when Black teachers knew their students from the community. Teachers in segregated schools and communities made sure that their kids could read. Families were involved with the schools and teachers before integration occurred. The county schools had less than the city schools after integration. Travillion, for example, was considered a county school.

"My advice for current or future teachers would be to try to stay focused. I would tell them to get to know each child in their room, and let children know they care about them. Kids respond if they know you care about them. I have taught three or four generations of families, and they knew how committed I was. Parents would request that their children be in my classroom because they knew how much I cared. If teachers demonstrate that they enjoy their jobs, and are strict, but love their kids, it will help everything. Go into work with a smile and let kids know where your heart is at. Celebrate with your students, like they are your own. Being a little personal and doing for kids like they are your own makes them want to learn. That is what Mrs. Fowler and my teachers growing up did for me. My teachers would celebrate with us, and we knew them from the community. Mrs. Heath, for example, was a role model for our entire community. There are so many people who looked up to her.

"I remember in 1964 we all went downtown to hear Dr. King and Jesse Jackson speak. We marched on the picket lines and marched with the Freedom Riders. I try to tell young people to vote. I tell young people to do their part. People like me worked to help younger generations have it better. I don't think some of the young people understand that. We had civil rights meetings at churches, and we worked to make sure that equality happened, even when the KKK threatened our lives. I would like to see more Black people vote. Go and vote—that is how we can continue to speak out! It is an honor to vote, and my childhood and upbringing taught me the importance of voting. I take it very seriously. I would also like to see parents participate in their kids' education. Staying involved with your babies' homework and school helps them get a good start and appreciate learning. I would like to see more young people finish school and go to college, because education is so important. We have to get young Black people to do better too. We can't complain about what whites won't let us do if we don't continue to work and get an education. Trade schools are also good options, and they can help people make good money. Education is never over with. There are always things you can learn.

"In the future I hope we see some changes in education. We need more Black teachers to go into teaching. If they knew how rewarding it is, I think they would understand this history better. I still get chills when I run into former students, and they tell me that I impacted their lives. It is the best compliment."[15]

• • •

Dear Future Educators,

My advice to you, first and foremost, is to have a passion for learning and a love for children. A smile can open a heart faster than a key can open a door. Smiles are free, so don't save them. Children love them because we never know what students have to go through in their lives or some homes or environments. Your classroom may be the only place where they get that love and acceptance. Love what you do, and it will make your days go so much better and easier. Remember that all children can learn. Remember that a smile brightens the world that we live in. Smile and be happy.

Sincerely,
Barbara Elaine B. Jones

Oral History of Mrs. Eleanor Deloris Goins
Educator and Principal, 31 years

Mrs. Eleanor Deloris Goins taught for thirty-one years in Hattiesburg Public Schools. She was a product of Forrest County Public Schools, graduating in 1964 from Travillion. She came from a family of eight children, four of whom went on to be teachers. She has three sons. Mrs. Goins is very involved in her community and grew up helping to fight for equality in the classroom and on the picket line. She was an active member of the Student Nonviolent Coordinating Committee (SNCC) and used her teaching and life as a means for activism. Today, she continues to work to preserve the history of Hattiesburg and remains involved in education and the community.

"In Hattiesburg between the 1950s and 1970s, the teaching profession was predominantly female, as most Black women became teachers,

Mrs. Eleanor Deloris Goins, educator.

secretaries, or nurses. The profession was gendered, but widely respected in the Black community. Black men were not prevalent as teachers from the 1950s to the 1970s. If they were present, they usually taught PE at the junior high or secondary schools. In the 1950s, teachers could teach without a degree. That later changed, and so Black teachers would go during the summer months to obtain specialist, master's, and bachelor's degrees.

"When I was coming up you could be a secretary or a teacher, and I chose to be a teacher to help others. I started teaching at Woodley Elementary. I also taught at Eaton and ended my careers at Grace Christian. I taught for a total of thirty-one years and saw so much. I enjoyed teaching and knew the importance of education. Black teachers brought tolerance, patience, determination that you were going to learn, discipline, and curiosity. They would make learning enjoyable and engaging. Not all children wanted to learn, but they didn't take no for an answer. You had parental guidance at home, and the neighborhood helped to raise me.

"I have always cared about standing up for equal rights, and I have always been so curious. In fact, I did not get my diploma the night of graduation. They had told us not to go to the picket line, but I went anyway. Mr. Todd told us that we could not attend graduation because of picketing the day before. I had an empty cover with no diploma. Imagine opening your diploma and moving your tassel on your cap, only to find out that there was no diploma! After graduation we were called into the office. It was a tactic to punish the Black students. Can you imagine not getting a diploma for standing up for what was right?

"The community suffered when integration occurred. The White Citizens' Council[16] would get their information from the Black community—the Uncle Toms—and they would use that information to cause harm. Thankfully, the Spirit[17] was a safe haven for mass meetings. Meetings would happen at Bentley Chapel United Methodist with Reverend JC Killingsworth. The community had to work to fight injustice, racism, and violence. The Spirit made sure that the community supported efforts for equality.

"White schools had state-of-the-art equipment, but the Black schools did not. We had old Bunsen burners in science class, and the teachers made do. Hand-me-down books, everything was hand-me-downs. Hand-me-down choir robes (colors of the school became green and white because they got the hand-me-down robes from Central (the white school)).

"We were not equal at all. We had dedicated teachers, though. I made sure to offer my students my dedication and time. I worked to teach the whole child. This meant we taught the entire child—socially, mentally, physically. I would use examples, hands-on learning, and teaching that took into account the different learning styles of students. The whole child approach also meant advocating for students, even when it went against the norm. I always went above and beyond what needed to be taught. Segregated schools lacked resources, but we at the very least had our respect.

"What can I say about integration? It was not easy. The white school leaders chose what they thought were the better Black teachers and put them in the white schools. Then, they chose the bad white teachers and put them in the Black schools—this is how we integrated. When we finally integrated, I found myself with students who were high performing. At the white schools, we were not given our history and white families were often against us.

"At the time we did ability grouping. Everyone that they couldn't handle they put in special ed—mostly it was the Black students. It used to just burn me up, because it would make students think they were less than. It was clear that there was a belief that Black students and Black teachers were not capable, and even with those of us who were supposed to be the 'good' teachers, they looked for reasons to get us out.

"I had a student call me a liar, and the principal said, 'Do you think him apologizing would matter? He won't mean it even if he apologizes.' The white mother came up to the school and told me that her son wasn't used to being talked to the way that she had been told I talked to him. The white principal sided with the family and did not support me at all as a teacher. That was one of the moments that I knew integration was going to really change things. Several teachers stood up and almost lost their jobs in the late 60s—1965. Teachers were involved in helping create equality, and many almost lost their jobs because of fighting for it. Mr. Heath, Mrs. Chambers, Dr. James, and Ms. Eleanor Harris all helped to fight for voting rights and equality. They wanted education and equal rights for everyone and were willing to risk their lives and jobs to help the cause. The Black trustees helped get Mr. Heath's job back.

"I've been on the picket line for civil rights, for teachers' pay raise. The state of Mississippi paid white teachers way more than Black teachers. Now, Mississippi has a great retirement system with a thirteenth check every year in December. We didn't get paid in the classroom though, and the salary schedule started when integration did. When I first started teaching in the 1960s, the pay was $315.82 a month. Teaching was an act of love. I am still very involved in the community, and I try to help mentor the teachers who are coming up."[18]

• • •

Dear Reader,

    I, Eleanor Deloris Goins, was born and raised in the city of Hattiesburg, state of Mississippi. I graduated from Earl Travillion Attendance Center High School in 1964. I am a Graduate of Utica Junior College, class of 1966, and Alcorn State University, class of 1968. I completed further study at the University of Southern Mississippi and William Carey University, respectively. My major was elementary education, with a minor in early childhood education. Prior to completing high school, I was involved in the civil rights movement. I was an active member of the Student Nonviolent Coordinating Committee. At the time I finished high school, I could not attend college in Hattiesburg. After completing my undergraduate degree, I returned to Hattiesburg and taught in the segregated schools of the Hattiesburg Public School system. In 1970 the schools were integrated. The so-called good Black teachers were sent to the white schools, and the so-called high achievers were also sent to the predominantly white schools. Integration wasn't easy for the teachers or the students. We felt then like we feel now with the latest ruling coming from the Supreme Court last week [*Students for Fair Admissions v. Harvard* and *Students for Fair Admissions v. UNC*, holding that race-based affirmative-action admission policies are unconstitutional]. The Constitution wasn't written to be used as it is being interpreted today. The Black students suffered a great loss then, and an even greater loss now. I shudder to think about the dreams I had as an educator during the sixties. We were making a difference, until things changed. I pray that in the near future we will consider what is best for our children, rather than what is best for our political and social agendas.

Sincerely,
Eleanor Deloris Goins

Oral History of Mrs. Mary Lewis Bobbitt
Special Education Educator, 30 Years

Mrs. Bobbitt came from a family of six girls and five boys and had a mother and father who made sure that learning was a priority and a rite of passage. At seventeen, she joined the Junior National Association for the Advancement of Colored People (NAACP) and stood in the picket line. Mrs. Bobbitt's mother hails from Shuqualak (pronounced sugar lock), Mississippi, and her father is from Aliceville, Alabama. Mrs. Bobbitt began teaching in 1968 and taught for ten years in special education at the elementary and high school levels. Mrs. Bobbitt loved teaching and loved her students and their families.

"I majored in special education, and I minored in elementary education. I started off as a second-grade teacher, and then the district decided I would move to special education, which I did, and that's where I stayed until I was out of the classroom. I had three-year-old students all the way up to age twenty-one. I found out quickly when they tried to tell us that separate but equal was okay. You know the inequities in schools didn't just happen in Hattiesburg. It was everywhere. It should not have been that hard to have equal and fair education for everyone.

"Education is so important, and I know this: my ancestors, my people felt a thirst for knowledge. Whatever is denied you, that is what you want. My mother grew up in a home where there were seven girls and two boys, and they were in Mississippi. After a certain age, they had to go to work. If they made it to the tenth grade, that was it, they had to work. It's not

Mrs. Mary Bobbitt, educator.

like they were getting married or anything, but they had a family to feed. So, everybody worked. It was the same way with my father.

"There were so many kids in the house.... My mother made a deal with the principal: if each child entering knew their ABCs, could count, and was able to read, the principal would allow them to begin school at age five. My mother valued education so much, she made sure that everybody in the family was assigned a child. The older kids would help get the younger child prepared and ready to go to school. That was your project for maybe a couple of summers—to make sure that baby brother knew the alphabet, how to count, how to write his name and address, and read certain sight words. So, I think Black families just had that thing inside of them. That education was the most important thing. We heard the word that education was power, and you saw families where if they had a lot of siblings, when one went to college and came out, then it was their duty to help the other one, not only with books but with tuition or whatever was necessary. It just became a family thing.

"I still think there are lots and lots of Black people who thirst for knowledge. There are a lot who are not given the opportunity. It's as if there has been a different route paved. Instead of from kindergarten to college, the route now is kindergarten to jail. There are many things in the environment that hinder Black success—for example, systemic barriers or poverty. This is the greatest thing that devalues people right now. When I was a kid, we could have been poor and everybody else could have been poor, but we didn't know it. There is a different kind of poor now. You know, it's the kind of poor when you do not have enough food to eat, when you do not have decent housing, even when you're not able to wash your clothes. That's a very different kind of poor than when I was a kid. You know, when I was coming up even though people said that they were poor, we were still feeding our neighbors when they were hungry. Poor does not always equate with just being hungry. You know, if you had a garden, you gave your neighbors what you had and shared with them. If you had corn in your garden, sweet potatoes, or tomatoes, you gave so many to folks all over the neighborhood, because that is what we did. We worked as a community.

"When I was seventeen, I belonged to the junior NAACP. Storytelling and activism were such important parts of my life. When I was a kid and my brother would tell stories, or my cousins or my mother, the stories were so vivid in my mind. And it was like, you hung on every word. The stories helped you realize things about the world. Storytelling was a truth, never questioned. It was a way of life, and it helped us understand activism. I look at the kids who are activists now, you know, I see the same people who walk the picket line with me, the young folk, and the old people, because it is just in our hearts that there is a better day. Things are not going to change unless I make them change, you know? And when I say 'I' it's not individually, but as a group—there are so many things you can do to make a change that does not involve walking a line. You can be an inspiration, you can send dollars, you can read. Even just talking to your neighbors because some of us become complacent and see it as somebody else's fight. If you don't remember, you won't know where you are going.

"As a teacher, I had a profession where you had to meet the children's needs, whether it was social, emotional, or physical. I've changed diapers. I've wiped snotty noses. I've cleaned up vomit. I've changed sanitary pads. I've cried when they cried because they couldn't participate in something because they were labeled as special education students. And the thing about it is, children know when they're being discriminated against whether it's ability-wise or whether it's color. The only thing I knew how to do was to just love them and meet them where they were and to do the best for them and spend a lot of time with the parents. If you're going to be a teacher today, make sure that is what you want to be. Because it's like a marriage, it's a lifetime commitment. If you are going to be there to help the children, to educate the children, you have to remember that you've got to educate the whole of the child. And sometimes that might mean educating the parents too.

"Special education was very much impacted after integration. What happens when Black kids move into a school district that is predominantly white? The preponderance of the Blacks, especially the boys, end up in special education or a behavior disorder class. Black and white students might have the same misbehavior, but the white child would remain in the class, and the Black child would get a label. Of course, I had started seeing this. I really think children, regardless, can learn better with someone that they identify with. You have to see people like you. At some point of time during the day, even if it's the cook or the PE teacher, children have to feel like they belong and that they're not just out there all by themselves. Because sometimes, all it takes is a smile to let a Black child know that he or she matters. Black female teachers bring more empathy and not sympathy into the classroom. There is a lot of encouragement for the children. I think we (Black teachers) are especially good at the empathy and the encouragement. We had no choice but to use skills like this, and our creativity. I used a lot of creativity in special education. If you cannot meet students where they are socially or emotionally, you really can't educate them. As long as we don't forget where we come from as Black teachers, we will always have a lot to offer to children. School integration did not fully change the hearts of humankind or improve the conditions of the disenfranchised in this country. Many children cannot truly engage with the education system when they are homeless, hungry, and invisible in this democracy called America.

"I would like others to know that I still enjoy the cards dealt to me in this life, as well as those opportunities that I have taken to benefit others."[19]

• • •

My children of this generation and future generations,

I want to let you know that this country is still evolving, and you are a very important product, essential to the growth of this country and of your people. It is not by chance that you are living at a time that is so trying in the lives of everyone; not only in this country but all over the world. Yes, there is turmoil, but there is also love and peace to be found.

My advice to you is to study and reach your full potential because this country and the world needs what you have to offer. Be proud of yourself and speak from your heart. It may seem that no one is listening to you, but they are listening. Speak up and speak out! There are many people out there ready and willing to aid and encourage you.

Please don't limit your vision. There are so many people out there who love you and respect you. Let them become a part of your journey: your family, your siblings, your neighbors, your friends, your teachers, and others who express an interest in you and what you do and what you want to do. Pay attention to those who are positive and ignore those who are negative and uncaring of your welfare.

I can share this with you: Black people have overcome many trials and tribulations and believe you me, we did not do it alone. We were guided by our elders, other young people, and our faith in God. I cannot tell you that it will be easy. There will be trials always, but we are overcomers. Reach for the stars each and every day. Expect a miracle every day. Whatever you do, do it because you believe in it. Others believe in you. Keep your eyes on the prize. It is waiting for you. It is meant for you.

As you climb, take others with you. I wish you the best in any and all of your endeavors and keep in mind that whatever God has for you, it is for you. All you have to do is take it. It is yours.

Sincerely,
Mrs. Mary Lewis Bobbitt

Oral History of Mrs. Linda Armstrong
Student at Forrest County Public Schools from 1949 to 1962 and Daughter of an Educator

Linda Sue Armstrong was born and raised in Hattiesburg. Linda was raised by her mother and father. Her mother, Mrs. Zola Jackson, was a teacher in Hattiesburg for thirty years. Her father, Mr. Alpheaus Bonard Jackson, was a laborer who worked at the Hercules plant in Hattiesburg, where he made bullets for firearms. She has two sisters and one brother. Growing up both as the daughter of a schoolteacher and as a student in Hattiesburg schools meant that she would be able to offer various perspectives in her oral history. Her perspective as a student on the impact Black female teachers had on her while growing up was important to include in this research, as it illustrates the impact that these teachers had on students in the community. Mrs. Armstrong grew up a lover of poetry and drama, theater, and journalism, and she would often gaze out the kitchen window while reciting poetry or daydreaming. She spent much of her time helping to maintain the household when her mother taught summer school.

Mrs. Armstrong attended segregated schools her entire life and shared her insights and experiences from that time as well as her thoughts about the connection between segregated schools and the Black community. She graduated from Earl Travillion Attendance Center in 1962 and left

Mrs. Linda Armstrong, student at Forrest County Schools.

Mississippi to attend college at Lincoln University in Jefferson City, Missouri that same year. Mississippi is a place that she considers to be stuck in time. Though her childhood was positive, she recounts knowing from a young age that Mississippi was problematic in creating unfair circumstances that impacted her.

"The schools were never integrated before I finished high school in 1962. I went to all-Black schools, all segregated schools, my entire school life. The teachers were capable of educating Black students. At school I didn't have to compete, and our school classes were very small in number. The teachers were very good and did things to the best of their abilities. They knew their purpose was to educate us, because teachers like my mom knew that whatever you did as a student you needed to be prepared to try to do better than the next student simply because you were not afforded the resources and opportunities that the white schools had. The white schools had foreign languages, we did not. So, when I got to college, I had no idea about Spanish class.

"Our teachers, they were on top of their education, and they kept up with their teaching license and learning. They went to college, it seemed like every summer, because they knew the resources and curriculum at the white schools were different. I know my mom had to go to Rust College in Holly Springs, Mississippi—that's where she graduated from—in order to keep her teaching license. Teachers had to renew their licenses if they wanted to continue to teach, so she went every summer to continue her learning. She had to be at a level equivalent to some of the other teachers. I think we had excellent teachers. I say excellent because they were caring teachers who worked to teach well. Black women were looked at as teachers, senior members, advisors, and guides who imparted knowledge. They were respected as vessels of knowledge who ensured that families stayed intact. This was an important aspect of our segregated schools and community. It was all I knew growing up, until I got to college.

"Our teachers cared about teaching the subjects and book learning, but they wanted to be sure that you knew and abided by—or try to at least—the golden rule, you know, to help others who are less fortunate than you. I know my mother was constantly taking a lot of our books and toys and all of that from home to give to students that didn't have them. We had more female teachers than male teachers, and it seemed like the male teachers we had specialized in something. I remember Mr. Clark, a male teacher who specialized in mathematics. We also had a male teacher who taught typing. The female teachers taught the more conventional classes, such as reading, writing, and arithmetic.

"My favorite teacher was Mrs. Craft. She was my fourth-grade teacher, and she was easy-going and easy to talk to. If she felt that you were behind or you could do a better job than you were doing in some of your studies, she would just kind of take you aside and tell you 'I know you can do better than this' and just say 'hey I'll give you, you know like, x number of days to get this right, or let us redo an assignment or something,' whereas my mom and some of the other teachers would just say you better get it done. But the teachers faced a lot. Black teachers weren't afforded all the supplies that were needed to sustain a classroom. And even though their salaries were at the bottom of the totem scale, in many instances they had to go out and buy much of their own supplies. If they wanted to help a kid as far as teaching them cursive writing, they had to buy pencils and I guess tablets, and a lot of extra books. I think a lot of the teachers did this—they had to supply a lot of their own materials for the classroom, because they felt that this would help the students succeed.

"I know my mom had a lot of Dr. Seuss books. My brother and I would sit on the floor and just crack up reading those books. We asked her how kids could learn anything with 'green eggs and ham' and 'Sam I am.' She told us it's because they're so silly that kids would remember the phrases. Mom was constantly buying books, and she just loved to hear people read. She would ask kids 'honey, what grade are you,' and she would sit right there and hold class, it didn't matter where we were. She was certain kids would learn when she was around.

"Teachers were prepared for class and things went as planned. Students were focused and there were not unruly students because we knew we were there to learn. The inside of the school and classroom was bland, but the unique aspect of the school was the fact that everyone looked like you. We were all in the same boat together. You looked forward to seeing these same faces every day—it was all we knew. Seeing faces that looked like you was empowering and added a sense of trust. A lot of us went to the same church, and you knew where everyone lived. We developed a strong sense of self because of the foundations we had at home, and the extension of that in the classroom. The teachers knew their jobs and their content and knew what they needed to do. They were always willing to go the extra mile and they exuded confidence in what they did, which transferred to the students.

"We all knew from the beginning that nothing about the schools was equal. And we knew then that nothing was equal as far as the materials, the books, or anything that we were getting. We were definitely shortchanged. I am glad I attended all-Black schools, though. We lived outside the city limits, and most of the white schools were what we call on the outskirts of the city, so there would have been no possible way for us to get there. Growing up, I didn't even know where white schools were. I think being in all-Black schools offered a sense of stability and cohesiveness. Of course, we also got that in our neighborhood. Some of the fellow teachers were our neighbors, and they were friends simply because my mom was a teacher. A lot of times, they would have get-togethers out in the yard and Mom would make ice cream. They were exchanging ideas, while the kids were maybe trying to establish rapport with some of the other students that we didn't see on a regular basis. I was comfortable with the people who I grew up with and who were in my community—I was accustomed to their manner of speaking, their behaviors, etc. Integrating with white students and white teachers would have been foreign to me. I am glad I finished my schooling before integration occurred. My high school graduating class had thirty-two people, so everyone knew one another, and the families knew each other. We functioned as a small family.

"If our teachers ever saw us doing wrong, they would tell the parents—you know, it was kind of like a chain of events if you did wrong in a classroom. There was no reason why some of the teachers wouldn't come by and let my mom know if I did anything. I'll tell you one incident: Our school used to let us go to shows a long time ago, like Western movies, but we had to catch the bus from school to get to the movies. I remember Bob Steele was one of the cowboys in those movies. A few times, my mother told us we couldn't go, but we went anyway. One time we got left behind—on the trip back to school, we missed the bus. So what are you gonna do? We had to call mom and daddy. That's the time you just want to run away, because you knew what was going to happen to you when you got home. The other teachers were telling them, 'Oh, your daughter went to see the movie and she got left behind.' It was an understood thing among the teachers that they would keep an eye on not only their own kids but on the other teachers' students. There was this great sense of community. Schools were Black, you know, and churches were Black. You could go for a walk and run into people in the neighborhood. There was a great sense of togetherness—in some families my mother taught three generations.

"There were a lot of single mothers, and some of the younger school-age boys felt obligated to help their parents out, especially if there were, say, several children in the family. Some people did miss out on their education because of family obligations. That's one of the reasons education was so celebrated, because we had to work through hardships. Black women had a large role in educating the community and the young people, whether they were teachers or whether they were just senior members of a church. They were constantly teaching and telling you about something that mattered. They helped instill a sense of what was right and what was wrong all the time. I think education did not necessarily come from a schoolbook or a college degree alone, it came from community. My mom would often say that sometimes you go to the school of hard knocks and learn simply by the mistakes you made in the past, and a lot of women, especially, played a big role in trying to help young people avoid some of the mistakes that they made. Black women were respected, and Black elderly women were respected simply because of their age and their position, whether they had a degree or not.

"When I left Hattiesburg, I remember reading that there were places that would say get out of Mississippi, don't fight the schools that don't want Black students, just go to a different city to get educated and come back. There were some junior colleges—my brother, for example, went to a school in the Delta. There were a few junior colleges in the state of Mississippi that Black students could attend, but not some of the major colleges at home, say, like the University of Mississippi. It seems like only recently since I left home that some of the Black students started attending William Carey College and some of the other local colleges, because at the time that I finished high school, I can't think of any colleges except some of the junior colleges in the Delta area—there was Mississippi State, there was Rust College. My first association and my first chance to 'rub elbows' with Caucasian students was at Lincoln, where I attended college. I didn't have any problems. I think as long as you treat people as human beings, and you treat them with respect, everything works out, but I am grateful for the insulated and excellent education I received growing up."[20]

• • •

To My Granddaughter and Grandsons and Future Generations,
    Congratulations! You are the voice and vision of our tomorrows. It will be an undaunting task for you because the struggles of past generations have led you to this day.
    There is an African word Sankofa (sahn-koh-fah), which means "to go back in order to go forward"—in other words, "go back and get it."
    Many of our ancestors were mistreated for various reasons: race, religion, and/or creed. Today, you have the knowledge and tools to "go back" and put down injustice, hatred, racism, antisemitism, and terrorism wherever it exists. Raise the flag to equality and brotherhood. Teach citizenship to all. You are the catalyst to right the wrongs where you find them, from the school room to the halls of Congress.

You will fulfill our expectations and our hopes. Why? Because our past has taught us not to accept things as they were, but to look to the future when things will be as they should have been all along—equality and justice for all!

Some of our great grandfathers, grandfathers, fathers, and brothers paid the ultimate price when they fought in various wars. The blood of our ancestors is embedded in the soil on many continents.

Many of us may not still be on this earth years from now, but remember, we are depending on you. Make us proud! Write your own stories for other future generations who will also "go back and get it." Your accomplishments and success will make your journey worth it; especially when you realize that we too embody the spirit of America.

Sincerely,
Mrs. Linda Sue Armstrong

Oral History of Dr. Joyce A. Ladner
Student at Forrest County Public Schools,
Educator, Sociologist, Author, Activist

Dr. Joyce A. Ladner is an activist, educator, sociologist, author, and former interim president of Howard University. Dr. Ladner grew up in Palmers Crossing in Hattiesburg, and she and her sister Dorie Ladner are known in Mississippi for working to advocate for equality and voting rights. She was mentored by Medgar Evers and Vernon and Ellie Dahmer, among others, and believes firmly in mentorship and the power of generational wisdom being passed down. She became involved with the NAACP and SNCC early on and has received many accolades. She taught at Howard University for seventeen years and remains an active force in the Black community today, advocating for equality. Dr. Ladner shared her beliefs about the importance of mentors, community, and Black educators.

"The *Brown* decision had an unusual impact on teachers. There was no rush to comply with the court decision. Instead, there was a rush to build new schools for Black students to stave off desegregation. The local white officials reasoned that if Black students had better schools like the white students, there would be no push to desegregate the schools. We got a new school at Earl Travillion Attendance Center, and schools that formerly served Black families in other parts of Forrest County bused students to Earl Travillion, with the students often passing white schools on the long bus rides. The *Brown* decision was like something over there someplace else because our teachers always focused on the students at hand. We were happy to have this new school with an indoor basketball court in the gymnasium. Earl Travillion had grades K–12. Segregation and inadequate facilities were two major factors that hung over the schools and the lives of teachers. They didn't mind that the schools were segregated. What they objected to were the inferior facilities and materials they had to teach from. All of the textbooks were used. They were sent to the Black schools after having been used by the white students for several years. You could see the names of the white students written inside the front of the book. No matter what condition the books were in, they were still sent to the 'colored' schools. We never had new school textbooks. Teachers often used their own resources for their classrooms. I told you that your [the author's] grandmother, Mrs. Zola Jackson, received a budget of $100 a year to buy books for the school library. When I started school in her class, the library consisted of one bookcase with books. I think there was also a set of encyclopedias. The public 'white' library was segregated. Later, in Earl Travillion, there was, I'm pretty sure, a real library but certainly not that

Dr. Joyce A. Ladner, educator, activist, sociologist. Photo by André Chung, 2023.

many books. Whether it was the library or clubs, teachers helped with all aspects of school life. Teachers used their cars to transport us to regional and statewide meetings of the New Homemakers and New Farmers of America meetings, the Hi-Y and Tri-Hi-Y [YMCA clubs for boys and girls]. I was the president of the Tri-Hi-Y club in 1960. Mr. and Mrs. Harper from Jackson, Mississippi ran it statewide, and one of our teachers served as the advisor. That club gave me important leadership skills, and the teachers helped to model what leadership looked like.

"What we didn't have in resources in school buildings, books, lab equipment, and sports facilities were compensated by the extraordinary investment of the human resources of teachers. My teachers were smart, and

> Post Office Box 69
> Palmers Crossing
> Hattiesburg, Mississippi
> October 12, 1959
>
> Mr. Medgar W. Evers
> 1072 Lynch Street
> Jackson, Mississippi
>
> Dear Mr. Evers:
>
> The interested young men and women of Hattiesburg have held their first meeting in the plans of forming a Youth Council in this area. There was a small group present at the meeting, however we realize that there is a great problem that the teenagers as well as the adults have. That problem is fear. We set up two objectives that we will try to carry out. They are: To stress the importance of unity among our race; To try to lessen the fear that our people have towards the opposite race and start a large membership campaign.
>
> We also feel that we can influence our adult branch to be more active. We choose our Nominating and By-laws and Constitution Committees. The group decided that the best date for you to come down is October 25, at 3:00 P. M. Our meetings will be held at True Light Baptist Church on Dewey Street. There are two persons that we have considered for our Adult Leader. They are Rev. W. D. Ridgeway and Mr. Clyde Kennard. We feel that Mr. Kennard will be more able to serve in the capacity because of the fact that Rev. Ridgeway is a Pastor. He probaly would not be able to give us his full time or as much as we would need. Both thought it was a very nice idea to form a Youth Council and both consented to give their time if we need them.
>
> If you will not be able to come down on the above date, please notify me as early as possible. Then give me a date that you can make, preferably Sunday.
>
> Looking to hear from you soon.
>
> Respectfully yours,
>
> Joyce A. Ladner

Letter from Joyce Ladner to Mr. Medgar Evers. Courtesy of Joyce Ladner.

they always had time for us. They knew they were working with fewer resources, and they compensated for it by giving of themselves. People forget that we had been living parallel lives with parallel institutions for years before desegregation, and so we made the very best situation we could to live and have enjoyable experiences.

"My education and learning experiences while growing up were good overall. My teachers ensured that we learned. I remember when my math teacher, who was very brilliant, found an error in the textbook. He wrote to the publishers, and they acknowledged that he was right and that they would correct it in the next printing.

```
                    October 16, 1959


        Miss Joyce A. Ladner
        P.O. Box 69
        Palmers Crossing
        Hattiesburg, Mississippi

        Dear Miss Ladner:

                    Congratulations on your first meeting, and
        I am very sorry that I was not able to be present.

                    It appears that the twenty-fifth will also
        conflict with a previous engagement that I have,
        which means that I will be unable to be with you at
        that time. The first Sunday in November is vacant,
        if that will be suitable for you, or any week day
        between October 26-October 30. Either of the dates
        will be fine with me provided you notify me immediately.

                    My personal acquaintance with both
        Rev. Ridgeway and Mr. Kennard influences me to say that
        either of the gentlemen would make a very good advisor.
        The choice, of course, is yours.

                    I shall look forward to hearing from you
        immediately.


                                Sincerely yours,


                                Medgar W. Evers
                                Field Secretary

        MWE:mes
```

Letter from Mr. Medgar Evers to Joyce Ladner. Courtesy of Joyce Ladner.

"I remember when my sister Dorie, who was a year older than me, missed a lot of days at school because Mother kept her at home to help with the washing and babysitting. My parents had six children younger than Dorie and me, so Mother had a very heavy load. The teacher came by our house to find out why she wasn't in school. That was the kind of teacher-student relationship we were accustomed to. I learned much later after I reached adulthood that Hattiesburg had the reputation throughout the state of Mississippi for having good schools.

"I attended DePriest School in Palmers Crossing from elementary school to my sophomore year in 1958. Our school was named for Oscar Stanton De Priest, who was an American politician and civil rights advocate from Chicago. DePriest School was built as a Rosenwald School in 1925, but nothing is left of it today except the cafeteria. In 1958, Earl Travillion Attendance Center replaced DePriest. It was a high school until 1969, when schools were desegregated, when it was consolidated and became an elementary school. The Black high school students were bused to what were primarily white high schools. I graduated in 1960, two years after Earl Travillion was opened.

"One of the most important things Black female teachers bring to students is empathy. They understand the challenges faced by Black students. They are willing to go the extra mile in helping students. In a lot of the schools in the South today, many of the teachers come from Teach for America. They are young and are not able to close the wide cultural chasm with the students. There are far fewer Black teachers today. I spent most of my career (seventeen years) teaching at Howard University, an HBCU (Historically Black College or University), by choice. I was dedicated to the idea that Black students needed professors like me to prepare them for life. I viewed my role as that of helping to develop the total person, and not simply to teach them what was in my syllabus. I viewed my role as a mentor, and I strove to be an excellent professor, like my own teachers in elementary, high school, and college had been. My activism was influenced by people like Vernon Dahmer, Clyde Kennard, Eileen Beard, Medgar Evers, my great-uncle Archie Betts, et al. The mentoring I received helped ignite my curiosity, activism, and learning. I knew it was my responsibility to help make the world better.

"I taught at a predominantly white college and an HBCU. I chose to teach at an HBCU (Howard), because as I often told my students, either by design or default, many of them, upon graduation, would end up working to make life better for Black people. I saw my role as preparing them to go out and influence other Blacks in a positive way. Race has always been central to who I am. I want to be remembered as a 'Race Woman,' like Ida

B. Wells and other notable Black women. The Black community and our teachers instilled in us what I call a 'can do spirit'—we were encouraged and empowered. Future teachers should approach teaching with the perspective of a lifelong learner, one who remains knowledgeable on the recent developments in her or his field. Teach students as if they are your own and use collaborative efforts to strengthen your teaching and the community."[21]

My time with Dr. Ladner offered insight into two perspectives: the perspective of someone who was an educator at the postsecondary level on an HBCU campus and the perspective of having been a student in Hattiesburg schools while growing up. At three and a half years old, Dr. Ladner would start kindergarten in my grandmother's classroom. Recognizing her curiosity and intellect, my grandmother would work to develop those qualities and would remind her that she had limitless possibilities. These initial lessons left an impact on Dr. Ladner and was one that she embraced and continued in her own teaching.

• • •

Dear Future Generations,

Here is my advice to you as you embark upon your future endeavors:

1. Follow your dreams and passions. All of us have dreams deep inside ourselves, and sometimes we don't follow those dreams because we take the easy way out. Figure out a way to do what you truly want to do. Dreams may seem farfetched to some, or they may raise questions in your own mind as to whether you can fulfill them but take a calculated leap of faith. You are always a better person if you fulfill your dreams instead of the dreams of others.

2. Put family first because that is where your lifelong identity and strength comes from. I remember once that my mother said, "There is no way I could ever disown one of my children." That stuck with me throughout my life because it speaks to the importance of how children are an integral part of their parents and families.

3. Embrace your inner self. There is a little voice inside all of us, and it speaks to us. No matter what is happening in the external world around you, always listen to that voice. Never silence your inner voice, because it is there for a reason, emerging from your subconscious. Listen to your internal monologue and learn to love yourself.

4. Hold on to your values. Your values will sustain you in good times and bad times. Values are the intersections of our past and the melding of what will enrich our future. Values hold together our families and communities, cementing one generation to the next. Values embody our faith and resourcefulness.

5. Take risks—whatever this means for you. Be courageous.

6. Value education and lifelong learning. Good teachers can unlock the love of learning. No matter how poor Black people were, we always believed in the power of education. My mother would say that "no one can take your education from you." Our ancestors and communities knew the power of education. There is great value in education. Lifelong learning is very, very critical because it keeps your mind engaged, satiates your curiosity, and makes you a better person. Education enhances your ability to communicate with people across generations. Learning never goes out of style.

7. Age gracefully and with abandon because age ain't nothing but a number. I consider myself ageless because I have always embraced change and lifelong learning. Ease into aging and lean into it. Aging can be a wonderful thing. It is a part of life, and age cannot define you. You are not in a fixed state; think of life as fluid and everchanging.

8. Travel widely. You may not have the means to travel but try to travel, nevertheless. Always be on the move, visit relatives, see the world, travel abroad if you can. Get outside of your comfort zone.

9. Never go against your first impressions. Explore and analyze the thoughts of your mind. Your first impression should be heeded or returned to, as it is often correct.

10. Love hard. Don't be afraid to fall in love. Love the people who deserve your love with vulnerability and your full self.

11. Believe in something outside yourself. Whatever God means to you, find it, believe in it—spirituality, nature, etc. It will be there for you in times of hardship. Believe in a higher power. Faith gives you hope and serves as both inspiration and a guide.

12. Be willing to give a helping hand. Embrace people of all races, faiths, and backgrounds. This might be hard to do in this polarized world, but it will serve you well and improve our world. Value all lives and help people who are in need. Earn your space in the world by giving back. It is the rent you pay for your space on earth.

13. Self-respect comes through respecting others. You learn early in life to have respect for certain things: life, liberty, others. Also learn to respect yourself along the way. Self-respect is a prerequisite to gaining respect for others and defining who you are. Self-respect helps cultivate relationships with others. Folks will treat you how you act, and self-respect is a cornerstone of this idea.

14. Life will be full of challenges. Some challenges you will meet head on, some you won't be able to meet, or you will decide not to meet. You cannot meet all of life's challenges, so prioritize where you give your energy.

These are the lessons and principles that I have learned from my own life and tried to live by. They have served me well; I am now sharing them with you now. You will undoubtedly have different principles and establish your own way forward. What is important is the ability to identify and apply values that allow you to live your best life. Go boldly into the journeys of your life. Your life belongs to you; it is important. Let your life shine through.

Sincerely,
Dr. Joyce A. Ladner

Oral History of Mrs. Carolyn Hale-Green
School Counselor, 25 Years

Mrs. Carolyn Hale-Green grew up in Hattiesburg, moved away after she got married, and then returned to Hattiesburg, where she resides now. Mrs. Hale-Green has her master's degree in counseling and worked as a school counselor for grades nine to twelve in Hattiesburg Public Schools. Mrs. Green retired after thirty-five years of service to the district.

"My first job was in 1968 at W.H. Jones, as a counselor. W.H. Jones was a Black school in Hattiesburg Public Schools. I was a counselor in 1971 when integration occurred in Hattiesburg. In 1971 I was moved to Hawkins (the white school) where I worked for two years until I was moved to Thames, which was a wealthy white school, where I spent sixteen years as a counselor. I also helped to sponsor the student council. I never had trouble with the Black or white kids, I was there to do my job and support students. At lunchtime though, I remember how divided it was—you could really see division. I also know that Black students had to work really hard for what they got. Even the way homework was graded was subjective. Black students had to earn it at the white schools, and even sometimes

Mrs. Carolyn Hale-Green, school counselor.

that was not enough. Black women in schools took an active role to try to make our Black students feel accepted, but at the white schools, that sentiment was no longer there.

"Black teachers had to take it upon themselves to advocate for basic rights, for the students, and for resources. Prior to 1971 there was not a salary scale, so school districts just paid you what they wanted, which meant Black teachers made less money than white teachers. Even meetings about retirement benefits were not meetings that we were invited to, so we had to advocate for that too.

"The white schools had books, fans, supplies, and resources, while the Black schools had none of these things. Black teachers had to really rely on getting something between your ears and into your brain. They focused on your learning, and knew they had to do it in ways that did not involve textbooks and typical resources, so to speak. Learning was always promoted by Black teachers, and Black excellence was expected and celebrated. All the Black teachers I encountered and worked with were great, especially the older ones. They had high expectations and knew how to work with students well. They were concerned about education and knew that they had a duty to do the best they could with what they were given. I could not imagine growing up with white teachers, because it would not have been the same. Growing up with Black teachers was a very important part of my learning and identity."[22]

Oral History of Mrs. Juruthin (Rosetta) Woullard
Educator and Principal, 37 years

Mrs. Juruthin (Rosetta) Woullard is from Hattiesburg, where she still resides. She taught for a total of thirty-seven years at the elementary level and was also a principal toward the end of her career. She was one of the first Black teachers, along with Mrs. Zola Jackson, to integrate Hattiesburg School District at Thames Elementary in 1971. Mrs. Woullard also described at length the success stories of students who emerged from Hattiesburg schools before integration, and the struggles faced by the students who were forced to attend integrated schools. Freedom of choice was something that impacted primarily the Black students who volunteered to integrate, while zoning and the implementation of a unitary district had a broader impact. In 1962, when Mrs. Woullard began teaching, the Hattiesburg Public School system had four schools for Black students (three elementary schools and one high school), and five schools for whites (three elementary schools, one junior high school, one high school). She said that her average class size was thirty to thirty-five students. She spoke proudly about her students who graduated from Black schools. Mrs. Woullard loved teaching and remains active by volunteering with the district and through her involvement with the Mississippi Association of Educators and FORDETRA (the local group that works to organize reunions and preserve local history mentioned above).

"I started teaching in 1962 at W.H. Jones Elementary School here in Hattiesburg. I taught fourth grade for eight years at W.H. Jones. During that period of time a seventh-grade English teacher got sick and was out for about five or six weeks. So, the principal of the elementary school put a substitute teacher in my place (fourth grade) and sent me to teach English to the seventh-grade students. The principal trusted me to teach at any grade level. After those eight years at Jones, we went into the beginning of integration and your [the author's] grandmother and I, along with about five other Blacks, were selected to go integrate Thames Elementary School (there were less than ten Black students at Thames). And so I stayed at Thames for eight years. And at the end of the eighth year, I had a call from the superintendent of Hattiesburg Public Schools asking me if I wanted to remain teaching at Thames or if I would like to go back to W.H. Jones to help set up a special gifted program for Blacks. It had never

Mrs. Juruthin (Rosetta) Woullard, educator.

been organized to set up, and the reason for that was because we had so many Black students who missed that original Reach Program, which was totally academics based, and they missed that program by one or two points. I was so thankful that they decided to organize another type of program for exceptionally bright kids.

"In the meantime, the principal at Thames said to me, 'Mrs. Woullard, I know that you have a choice to make and a decision. We would love to have you stay here at Thames. The parents love you. They're so pleased with you and how you are working with their children. They want you to teach the other children coming along. It is an honor to be asked to go, but there is no extra money in it, so it won't benefit you, um, monetarily, but you will be working to help organize a new program.' I thought about it and thought about it, and talked it over with my husband. And you know what I said—if I am good enough to stay there and teach those white folks' kids, if they want me there, well, I am good enough to go to back to my Black school and teach my Black children. Let them have my expertise, my time, and my teaching ability. And I went back to the Black school (W.H. Jones) and helped set up that program. It was a beautiful program. You had to qualify for it by being exceptionally bright with music, dance, singing, or art. I said, you know, I want to go and help my Black race. So, I went back, and the program lasted eight years. I was the only Black teacher left in the program. I was the only one of the original ones left in the program.

"I want to say we integrated in 1971, and when we integrated, Mrs. Zola Jackson and I are probably the only Black teachers that went to Thames because it was the prestigious, all-white school. There were other schools, but this is the school closest to the university. And we had lawyers, doctors, and university personnel all attending Thames School, so they picked who they thought were the 'best' Black teachers, and that caused some problems. We felt honored to be asked by the superintendent to help integrate, but other Black teachers were not so lucky. Now they had the other white schools, they sent Black teachers to those schools also—they were sending the best of the crop to Thames. They sent white teachers to the Black schools.

"We have often said that our children did not succeed as much with white teachers as they did with Black teachers. We as Black teachers could understand where our children were coming from. We understood, we had to teach and needed to teach the whole child because we were their parents away from home. Let me stop there for a moment . . . speaking about parents, parents away from home. I told my white kids this, because I was used to telling my Black children this. I told my white kids I was their mother away from home. Boy, they sat up, straight back, and looked at me funny. I said, think about the number of hours you are with me, actively working, learning, and then you eat here. They relaxed a little! Oh, I see where she's going. She doesn't mean that she's my mother! I thought that was so funny. We had to change some of the phrases we used and the way we talked. . . .

"I have always believed in teaching the whole child. You teach them about personal hygiene and good health and good manners and, you know, things other than the skills from the textbook. You have to teach the whole person, and that's what I've always tried to do for my Black students and white students. A lot of times, if white teachers did not know how to discipline our Black children and acted as if they were afraid of them, the kids could read through them and see that. You've got to know the child and find a way to work with them and understand them. So, it takes more than textbooks. I always tried to give the person honor, because it really does take a village to raise a child. When we were segregated, people on our street in the community could chastise us, get on us if we were acting up, coming home, or going to school. And, God forbid, if you got in trouble at school and you had to be disciplined, honey, the kids in the class would beat you home telling their mom, and then going to tell your mom. So, we got it from the teacher, we got it from parents on the street, and then we got it when we went home. So that's taking the best ways and having the people in the community to work with you and your children too. But nowadays, it is different.

"Of course, at the beginning of the integration, you still had white parents who really were not partial to their children being taught by Black teachers. Some of them pulled their children out and put them in private school or would have them study at home—white flight is what they call it. Some of them did flee. Some of them I remember distinctly went to Oak Grove, that Benson area outside of Hattiesburg that's still a part of Hattiesburg. And, at one point in time, Petal was a part of Hattiesburg, but they pulled out and became a city, and some of them would find relatives to send their children to school in Petal.

"I focused on my job because I've always been one who wanted to do the best job I could possibly do, whether it was my first eight years of teaching or it was the next eight years with integration. And I tell you also that as teachers, we were sort of on edge. We felt like, you know, we had to be very careful because some things we could say to Black kids, white kids didn't understand. Sometimes a phrase might come out that you were used to saying to Blacks that the whites didn't understand. And of course, they went home and told their parents, and the parents called the principals, and the principals would let us know, at the end of the week.

The principal would call all the Black teachers in, and he would say, 'Be careful, be very careful. We know this is an adjustment for you, but you've got to learn how things are here. How you say things, how you said things at your former school you can't say here at Thames.' He wanted to make sure things went smoothly.

"There was a teacher for every grade. And, if there were two sections of fourth grade, there was a Black teacher for each section. And then when there were four classes, there may have been two Black teachers, because some of the classes were large.

"I know that after integration, there was the fact that Blacks were determined to find their place because before we integrated, we had Blacks here in Hattiesburg graduating with honors. And, we had Blacks that happened to finish eleventh or twelfth grade to go to college—this is before integration. And so, after integration, Blacks had a hard time trying to excel over a lot of the white race. But they worked hard and had they been in an all-Black school, they would have succeeded. But after integration, you know, they [the white teachers and administration] were going to put their own race at the tip top. Now that doesn't matter so much, if Blacks have earned it, because people have realized that some Blacks are just as smart as whites. And so you have Black valedictorians and salutatorians of these schools. And I tell you, one young man who went to Rowan did not attend eleventh and twelfth grade but went to college and ended up with his doctorate degree. Dr. Walter Massey is his name, and he was in the area of math and chemistry. He is well known by chemistry professors and all. He's a product of Rowan, um, Royal Street. It was Royal Street when he was there. It became Rowan.

"We used to say integration hurt us. If we had continued without the integration, students more than likely would have excelled. They would have had their own Black teachers, but the thing of integration was that they had so much new material, updated materials, equipment, and all of that. While our children benefited from that, we had white teachers telling kids, 'you will never make an A in math in my class or don't even think about being a lawyer.' Our people really weathered the storm.

"When we were segregated, we got some equipment, but we didn't get everything that the white school had in their biology labs or chemistry labs. We got what was given to us or what we purchased. Let me go back to my earliest years of teaching—and it didn't just happen with me. But a lot of, most of, the Black teachers were of course given hand-me-down books to teach our children and no workbooks at all. So, if we did buy workbooks, if we didn't ask parents to help us sell items, there were a lot of things we didn't have. They just didn't give the Black schools resources. So, we took it upon ourselves, being as resourceful as we wanted to be and could be, and we purchased things for ourselves. I remember a second-grade teacher—I was two doors down from her when I first started to teach. She had one of those old duplicating machines that you would pour ink into, lay the full pan on top of the ink and press it down, roll it. That's how duplicate copies were made. And she purchased that machine with her own money. So, a lot of things that we had to work with, we purchased with our own money because we love teaching. We love working with students.

"The mayor of Hattiesburg for sixteen years came from W.H. Jones. We have had supervisors come from the Black school. We had our first Black councilman who attended W.H. Jones. These people were brought up through segregation, and they did well and became very successful. I think that is because of the care Black teachers offered to their students. Integration, you know, has its role and that I would say it enhanced resources because of the extra materials and new equipment. However, our people had to get used to that education and the difference in teachers.

"I definitely think Black female educators played a very important role in educating Black students. I had one female educator who played a very important role in my life. In fact, when I talk about my mentors, she is one of them, other than my mother. She was a fourth-grade teacher and fourth-grade principal at the same time. That's what they did for our Black schools. And when they added fifth and sixth grade, they moved her to teach sixth grade. She was my sixth-grade teacher. She was my fourth-grade principal, she still had dual roles, and she would teach us, she taught the whole child. She would make sure our faces were washed and clean. She checked our ears. She looked at our feet and made sure our shoes were nice and neat. She really taught the whole child. She was so good, and people looked up to her. I know I did. So when I graduated from Tougaloo College and wanted to teach, she wrote a letter of recommendation for me. I turned that letter into the superintendent, they put it on file, and I was hired. Her name was Mrs. Lillie M. Burney. Not only did I have the privilege of going to that school as a student when she was my principal, but I had the privilege of being principal of the school they named after her. I also had the privilege of teaching in that school for thirteen years. I taught for a total of thirty-seven years and I loved it, but I knew it was getting time for me to move on, so I prayed and asked the Lord to let me know when it was time for me to retire. The Lord let me know when it was time to go. And I received that blessing. Teaching was such a blessing.

"I can say the Black community has truly come a long way. There are many people who can really relate to picking cotton in the fields—having to go to school half the day and pick cotton half the day. I didn't have that experience. I was not too far from Rowan where I went to school, so we walked to school and some of us could come home for lunch and then go back to school. I was blessed to have my mother, who finished twelfth grade and was very active. She was even a PTA president, and she made sure that we were engaged in activities. So, what I'm trying to say is that I didn't have experience working in the cotton fields. And in fact, in Hattiesburg, we didn't have cotton fields, they were up in the Delta. As I said, I have heard friends and people talking about having to go to school a half day, living on plantations, who had to pick cotton in order to survive. I would teach a lot of units to my students about history and Mississippi history."[23]

Oral History of Mrs. Katherine Fowler
Educator, 44 years

Mrs. Katherine Fowler was born in a rural part of Covington County in Mississippi. Her husband was also an educator at Earl Travillion School. Mrs. Fowler taught for forty-four years in Mississippi. She taught home economics throughout her teaching career to grades four through eleven. Her career included teaching at Covington County Schools, Mt. Pleasant, and Stone County. She taught at the Black schools both before and after the *Brown* decision and during desegregation efforts after 1970. She has

Mrs. Katherine Fowler and Mr. Fowler, educators.

four girls, and she lost her husband when one of her children was only four years old. Her husband was a respected teacher at Earl Travillion. Together, Mrs. and Mr. Fowler dedicated their time and lives to educating and mentoring students.

"I always wanted to be a teacher. When I was little, we would meet under a tree and play school. In different ways, I have always been a teacher in my home and community. The community helped raise and educate the children. In most communities, the parents respected the teachers and principals, so there were not problems in the classroom. If parents did not support you, it created problems. If children could not behave, you gave them three licks with a twelve-inch ruler to get them in line. After integration, this could not occur, so classroom management and respect were just a few of the things that changed.

"Mississippi did all it could to delay integrating its public schools. In the Hattiesburg Public Schools, it was common practice for Black schools to receive the worn, tattered schoolbooks from the all-white schools. After the books were so badly worn, they would be rebound at the state penitentiary and stamped with 'Parchment Penitentiary' inside the books. Can you imagine the impact of seeing the name of a correctional institution inside your educational books daily? It's almost too much to imagine.

"Integration had a great effect on the Black community, and most of it was negative. The churches and schools had a positive impact on the Black community, so that helped. Teaching was organic in the community; it was viewed as something that happened naturally. Students and teachers came together, worked together, to make voter registration happen and make the community better. The community would lift each other up, especially through difficulties. We as a community always found ways to have enjoyment—a cookout, laughter. I thank God for that.

"I think integration had a great influence on how few Black teachers we see today. Teachers were not really looked up to in the Black community after integration. Choosing to become a teacher in an integrated school came with the different ways people looked at it. There was also the bad blood that happened in the Black community when the 'good teachers' got asked to go to the white schools. This caused dissention among Black teachers and changed the cohesion that was there before integration.

"After integration, some Black teachers were overly concerned about being accepted. We called them Uncle Toms—you had to treat 'em with a silver spoon. You had to unspin them from the narrative and track that they had been led to believe. I talked about the positive impact the churches and schools had on the Black community, but in some ways, it could not compete with the damage integration caused. Black folks were so worried about keeping up with the whites that they lost some of their priorities and themselves—they would go along to get along.

"I remember the first run-in I had with a white parent at the integrated school—I was on a break, and the parent came in on my break and started coming closer and closer to my desk. She was so aggressive and was upset because her child had told her that I was mean to her. I tried to talk to her, but she had made her mind up and had no intention of believing a Black teacher. I talked about how integration changed the respect for teachers and principals. Teaching went from being a respected profession to one that was not due to all of the politics involved. Teaching was respected when it stayed within the community, but after integration it became more about giving up who you were to please white people.

"Black teachers had to be so particular and careful about what was said to the white kids and families. Before integration this didn't happen, so these problems didn't exist. Integration also changed what was taught and how teaching the lessons was approached. For example, Black history was taught in the Black schools, but at the integrated schools it was only acknowledged during Black History month. That was such a shame. So many things changed."[24]

Oral History of Mrs. Jemye Heath
Educator and Principal, 43 Years

Coincidentally, I had met Mrs. Heath many years ago in Hattiesburg and spent time in her home, as my momma insisted that we pay a visit to her favorite teacher. Her house was comfortable, pictures everywhere, the television as background noise as my momma and aunt talked with her for hours. Before leaving, I took photographs of the three of them together, to mark the moment. At the time, I did not realize how important that moment truly was. I do now. Her story marks the beginning of my journey into this history.

Mrs. Jemye Heath was born and raised in Hattiesburg. She lived to be ninety-nine years old and spent a total of forty-three years teaching. She recalled that she always wanted to be a teacher from the time she was a little girl and played school with her dolls. Her experiences teaching in Hattiesburg were mostly positive, despite the hardships she endured. She taught both third and sixth grade, which included teaching all subjects. She was a principal for the last six years of her career. Teaching at all-Black schools is how she began her career and taught for many years, until she was forced to move to the white schools after desegregation. Education runs deep in her family, as her husband William Heath was a school principal. Despite the hard times she endured, teaching was something she wholeheartedly loved and enjoyed. It was an honor to have heard her story.

"I have always wanted to be a teacher, ever since I was little. We would play with dolls, and I would say to people, I am going to be a teacher someday. I wanted to be a teacher ever since way back, and here I am, a retired teacher now. I taught for thirty-two years. I lived in Hattiesburg and got married. We both worked at the school for years, and then after integration, you had to sign a form if you belonged to the NAACP. My husband signed the form, and they fired him. We had to move to the Delta, and that was a struggle. We had three children, and it was bad, no money and no jobs. We ended up picking cotton and renting a house from the man who owned the plantation.

"Later, we ended up moving back to Hattiesburg. My husband worked for twelve years as a principal. I taught sixth grade and then third. Most of my teaching was at the elementary level, third grade. There were usually

Mrs. Jemye Heath, educator.

at least twenty-five students in a room, and the teacher was the one to create the lessons.

"When schools first integrated, I was the first one to be moved to an integrated school. They moved me from sixth grade down to first. In the first faculty meeting, a white teacher said to me, 'You remind me of my maid.' I told her, no, I am not that. So, I knew right away it was not going to be easy to work with her. I went to the principal and told her exactly what the white teacher had said. I said, 'I don't feel comfortable here. I don't want to work with first grade, because I don't feel comfortable with that teacher.' So, they assigned me to third grade. I guess they thought we didn't know anything because the administrators and principal would come to my room often to peek in and see what I was doing. Another Black teacher that taught with me got in trouble for saying something to a student that he didn't like. They fired her right on the spot. There was always the fear of losing your job or not being treated fairly by the white teachers. I had three teachers that worked close to me, but most wouldn't even come into the room if I was there. Some would act as if they didn't see me.

"I want students today to learn about voting. I would tell young people to finish college. I would tell them my story. I would tell teachers today to respect their education and be creative. I want teachers to learn to work together. Teachers need to know how to make a difference in children. Treat students equal. Treat them fair. You can make a difference in children by getting to know them and loving them. Children know when you love them. The main thing is to get those kids to respect you and love you. If you get the children on your side, you can get the parents to work with you, too.

"Teachers in my day were smart, able to do expert things with very little, and they created great activities where the children could learn hands-on. I would tell teachers today to be curious because you learn from asking questions and whatnot. Teachers should not always do stuff in the textbooks. What you have to do, you know, is create things. I'll tell you what I used to do. I would get magazines about everything—science, history, and on Fridays I would take that to class and tell them, we are going to travel today. We would use the magazines and lessons to go to the beautiful countries in those magazines and learn about them. I would integrate that with my teaching. It takes more than the textbook.

"For example, I think our Black children need to know more about Black heritage. Now there is so much equipment and whatnot, and some of the companies that schools get books from need to change. There is all this technology now, but what is being taught isn't advanced. If we want education to be its best, we need to get together and talk more about different things—you learn from that. If you come together and work together and mean what you say and ask questions, it tends to work out.

"I was a little leery when integration happened. When they said we had to integrate and told me I *had* to go to the integrated school, I was worried. I didn't want to go. I asked my husband what I should do, and he said 'Go, teaching children is why you are a teacher. Don't lose your job, go over there and teach as well as anybody else.' So that's what I did. I wanted to teach and help kids. There were good and bad white teachers at that school. I found a few I was able to mingle with. I have always used my voice and spoken up for myself, even when it was hard. Sometimes you have to step out on faith. I would say what needed to be said and have faith that it was going to be all right. I said things from my heart, stood up for my beliefs, and it usually served me well.

"The world is a mess now, and teaching is hard. When I first started teaching, I made $60 a month, and then after I got my bachelor's in science, I got up to $1,400 a year. When my husband retired, he was making about $15,000 a year. When I retired, I was making $22,000 a year. I've been retired now for eighteen years. The relationships and the experiences were worth the low pay most of the time, but teachers should be paid more money, because real teaching takes creative thinking and the ability to respect all children."[25]

Oral History of Mrs. Zola Jackson
Educator, 37 years
Told by Mrs. Linda Armstrong

Mrs. Zola Jackson began teaching in 1944 and taught in Hattiesburg for thirty-seven years. She taught in both Hattiesburg Public Schools and Forrest County Public Schools. She was the wife of Alpheaus Jackson, and together they had four children. She was a member of the Mount Olive Baptist Church, a Sunday school teacher, a member of the Mission Society, and she helped teach Bible study classes at a nursing home. She was a small-framed woman, with stylish glasses that showed her high cheekbones, and she always wore earrings. Despite her petite stature, she was full of verve and determination. Her daughter Linda Armstrong described her as the "baddest little woman in Hattiesburg."

"Mrs. Jackson did not play when it came to education and high expectations, and she had a reputation for being strict. She was outspoken, bold, and creative. Her stature could've misled others to underestimate her spirited demeanor—she meant business and when teaching in the classroom, she was no nonsense. After all, she had gone to great lengths to receive her own college education, saving bit by bit and then traveling hours to Rust College to become a teacher. She knew the importance of reading and writing, and she expected her students and children to respect its power. When her school lacked a library and resources for books, she created a library, furnishing many of the books with her own money, and volunteering to help students check out books. She would bring home piles of books to us [her children] as well, many of which were Dr. Seuss books, because she said the 'silly words and rhymes made kids want to keep reading.' We despised the Dr. Seuss books, and would scoff at *Green Eggs and Ham*, fidgeting as she read them aloud. No matter, she kept reading, tapping her knee once to demand our attention. We recalled the books that we did enjoy, which included *Little Women*, *Robinson Crusoe*, and *The Littlest Angel*—these books were read on repeat in the Jackson household. Zola would even write inside the leaf of the book 'Children, take care of your books!'

While out buying groceries or in the community, it was not uncommon for Zola to approach children to inquire about their reading or writing skills. She'd say, 'Baby, can you read?' Depending on the answer, she

Mrs. Zola Jackson, educator.

might clear a space to hold school right then and there. When we pleaded, 'Momma, school is out, can we go home please?,' she'd give a look, and we knew that her response would be 'this is too important, and it cannot wait,' and so we would wait and wait and wait, for as long as it took for her to teach a lesson. These interactions often led to her keeping up tutoring or teaching sessions in her home, because literacy, as she often mentioned, was 'the key to maintaining freedom.'"

Mrs. Zola Jackson leaves a legacy behind that was rooted in acceptance and love for all students and high expectations. She believed that it was important to take the time to listen each individual student. No matter the challenge, she thought all students could learn and were capable of achievement. Her career was dedicated to helping create possibilities for her students and the community—whether it was making a home visit, gifting a book to her student, making homemade ice cream, or mentoring, she worked to make certain that students felt challenged, affirmed, and valued.[26]

Oral History of Mrs. Ellie Jewell Davis Dahmer
Educator, 38 Years

Mrs. Ellie Jewell Davis Dahmer received a bachelor of science in home economics from Tennessee State Agricultural and Industrial College in 1947, and an elementary education certification from Jackson State University. She taught in Jasper County, Jones County, and then Forrest County. Mrs. Dahmer's husband is the late Vernon Dahmer, and they had eight children (seven boys and one girl). The Dahmer family had a farm where they grew cotton, corn, peanuts, and sugarcane. In addition, the family owned a grocery store. Mrs. Dahmer was one of the first to be able to register to vote in Hattiesburg, and she later served as the election commissioner for three years. She is a lifelong advocate for academic achievement, literacy, and voting.

"I started teaching home economics in Bay Springs School in 1948. While I was at Bay Springs, they changed principals, and the principal hired his wife to take my position, so I had to attend Jackson State to take courses in English and social studies so I could teach those subjects. Later they needed a teacher in Hattiesburg, so I interviewed and went to work there. I taught a total of thirty-eight years. During the time we were segregated we got all of the old books and encyclopedias. We didn't know what a new book looked like. My husband (Mr. Vernon Dahmer) was very active in the NAACP. After his involvement in that, the schools refused to hire me in the county. All of the Black schools were consolidated into one school, in Palmers Crossing, and the schools and principals had a list of names, of who not to hire, and my name was on that list. I ended up getting a job at Richton school system (a city school) where I stayed for twenty years. It was segregated initially and then became integrated in 1970 and 1971.

"As educators, we worked to teach the children everything. We knew that students would have to compete with children from other schools. We taught them how to dress, how to speak, and how to carry themselves in general. We taught all Black history in the segregated schools and then could not teach it at the integrated schools.

"Hattiesburg is a wonderful place. We have two four-year colleges that were integrated, and several that are two-year colleges. Integration gave us new buses and new books, so we were able to enjoy those things. I viewed integration as a positive thing. I think integration helped the Black community, because we got to enjoy some of the things we had always paid for with our tax money. It improved the atmosphere.

"My advice to future teachers would be teaching the child where you find them at and bring them up to the standard they should be at. Students

Mrs. Ellie Jewell Davis Dahmer, educator. Photograph by Andrew Feiler, andrewfeiler.com, from the book *A Better Life for Their Children*. Shared with permission of the photographer. Ellie Dahmer was a teacher at Bay Springs School in Mississippi and the wife of civil rights activist Vernon Dahmer.

have a phone and computer, so they can find any information they want to know. I think all history should be taught in schools. We tried to improve the students in every way. We tried to teach them how to live with other people. I loved teaching math and fifth and sixth grade. I taught all of the classes in fifth and sixth grade. Richton was a small school and there were multiple grades in one classroom. Most city schools were considered the good schools and the county schools were not [for example, Mr. Cooper shared that county schools such as DePriest did not have indoor bathrooms, while the city schools did].

"Most of the time teachers were respected in their profession and in the community. I had a wonderful teaching experience. I stayed in Richton so long that I taught many generations.

"I would like to tell everyone to get a college degree. We want all students to take some type of training. If you are not interested in a four-year degree, get a trade so you can better your living condition. There is no excuse not getting one now. I had one in 1947. There was no such thing as financial aid, and I did it. I also want others to know that voting is important. We need to make the choices in who will make decisions for us. Go vote."[27]

• • •

Letter to students of today,

My name is Ellie Jewell Davis Dahmer. I grew up in a rural farming community in Jasper County, Mississippi called Rose Hill. My father, Sam Davis, was literate. My mother, Bettie McMillian Davis, had poor literacy skills. My mother instilled in me the need to obtain the ability to comprehend for myself. My parents and grandparents donated land for the local Methodist Church. As a child my early education through the seventh grade was at Wesley Chapel United Methodist Church. White students had several schools in Jasper County. My parents donated land that the school for Negro children was built on in 1939. I graduated from Jasper County Training School in 1943.

Attendance for some of my classmates was sporadic depending on their family's living situation. If their family "lived on someone's place" as sharecroppers, the children's education was not the first priority. The elders of my church encouraged all members to buy a place of their own. Sharecropping is part of Mississippi's Jim Crow systematic approach to thwart the advancement of Black people. The majority of today's students have no knowledge of who or what Jim Crow was. Separate but equal was never equal in Mississippi.

Today's students should take advantage of all educational opportunities available to them. Library cards are free. Get one and use it. Reading is the basis for further education. Students should know that less than 1 percent of high school graduates will become professional athletes.

The small group that does "go pro" will need to comprehend what their contracts entail.

Precious blood has been shed and lives have been taken in order for Black people to have the rights we have today. Register and vote. Encourage your peers to do the same.

I worked two jobs on campus as a dishwasher and custodian in the single female living quarters while attending Alcorn College in 1943 and 1944. There were no grants or scholarships available to me at that time. Apply for all educational assistance that you can. Start your postsecondary education at a community college. They are always cheaper.

Postsecondary education is not a desire or option for all. The vocational path can provide young people a means to live comfortably and contribute to our community.

If you go online or go to a library and educate yourself about all of the racial disparities that have been inflicted on Black people because of a civil war, state legislation, federal legislation, or the Supreme Court, you will comprehend the value of an education. Remember the slave owner could beat a slave, rape a slave, abuse a slave in any manner, sell a slave away from their family, and it wasn't against the law. It was only illegal to educate a slave.

We are no longer slaves. No one is going to murder you or your family if you register to vote. Own where you live. It's time for you to do YOUR PART.

Retired Educator of 38 years,
Ellie Jewell Davis Dahmer
Tennessee Agricultural and Industrial College

HISTORICAL VIGNETTE

Christopher M. Span

The Resilient Story of Why We Are Here Today

The journey of how we arrived at this moment today is a tapestry woven with choices—choices made by individuals facing unimaginable adversity, choices that shaped not only their own destinies but also the trajectory of future generations. Often, when we reflect on history, we question why more wasn't done, why action wasn't taken sooner. Yet, we fail to recognize the revolutionary nature of choosing resilience in the face of oppression.

Consider the harrowing journey of Africans captured and transported in the hulls of slave ships. Amid the unspeakable horrors, they faced the choice to surrender to despair or to persevere. Similarly, those who endured the brutality of plantation life confronted daily decisions—to flee, to resist, or to endure. It was these choices, seemingly small yet actually monumental, that paved the way for the existence of future generations, including ourselves.

In acknowledging our past, we must honor not only the known leaders of revolts but also the countless unnamed individuals whose legacies endure through oral tradition. Their stories, passed down through generations, offer a glimpse into the resilience and empowerment that defined survival in the face of unimaginable hardship.

The history of America is intertwined with the history of slavery, but the true essence lies in how African Americans survived and thrived within that institution. Slavery is American history writ large; how enslaved people survived this horrid period of American history defines African American history. This narrative often eludes written records but is preserved through the oral histories shared by elders. Through these stories, we gain insight into the nuanced complexity of choice—the choice to endure, to resist, and ultimately, to shape a future where freedom reigns.

As we seek to retrace our roots and understand our collective history, we must heed the wisdom of our elders. Engaging in conversations with grandparents and great-grandparents allows us to unravel the threads of our ancestry and gain a deeper understanding of who we are. It is through these conversations that we unearth a counternarrative to traditional records, offering a richer, more nuanced perspective on our past.

So, when we contemplate the choices made by our ancestors, let us do so with gratitude and humility. For it is their resilience, their determination, and their unwavering commitment to survival that has brought us to this moment today. And in acknowledging their journey, we find a roadmap for understanding ourselves and shaping a more just and equitable future.

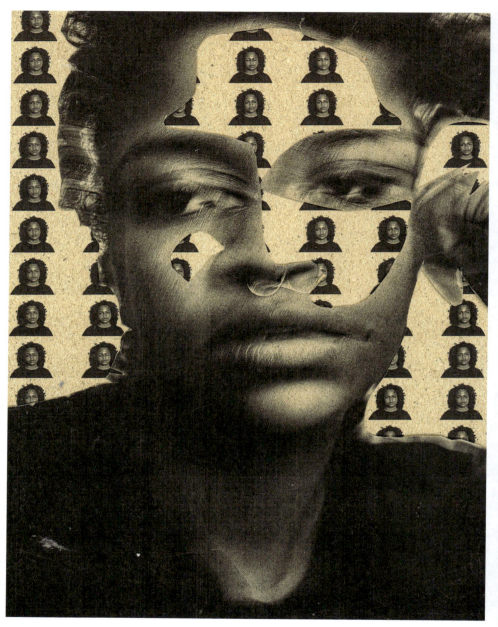

Rebecca Marimutu, *Contact #98*, 2022. Archival pigment print. "I see a connection between this book and my work, as I focus on how the Black woman is represented and expanding how Blackness can be represented in photography."

POETIC REFLECTION

On Caskets[28]

Nate Marshall

After Suji Kwock Kim

1

decorating the dead is among the most basic
human instincts, to return the borrowed body &
acknowledge Earth as maker & home.

Neanderthals used antlers & flowers. Egyptians
had pyramids with peasants buried in the walls they
built. Some niggas just get a pine box. Hopefully
you get a hole or a flame. Some only get a cold
cabinet in the morgue until somebody or nobody
claims them as a loss.

2

a permanent fixture on my to-do list
is research life insurance plans. Pick
a good one with a fair rate & enough
money to buy a nice box.

3

*everything gonna be all
right this morning* & I contemplate
the implications of the statement for the night.
Everything in Mississippi is too cruel to bury.

I wonder what that means if every body in Chicago
has red clay in its lineage. Chief Keef must know
in his bones *ball like it's no tomorrow* from what
Muddy time-capsuled into the South Side ground.

4

when grandma died she left mama a notepad
with instructions. The one I remember was *get
the casket you want. What you like. Don't be
pressured.*

We wore blue at the service. We matched
the box & its glossy painted ribbons,
gold-flecked & light.

5
house slaves are responsible for preparing
the dead of the master's house. They clean
& clothe. They dig the hole. They don't
bury any black body really, only dispose.
One of the concessions won by slave riots
was the right to a funeral. Whitefolk were
confused at how the Africans sometimes

wore white, smiled, shouted like joy.
They seen funerals. Not homegoings.

6
my mother used to say my father loved
funerals. He worked graveyard shift & spent
the days & weekends visiting bodies.
Running his finger alongside the box
& signing the greeting book.

The most decent thing you
can do is visit the funeral of
someone you didn't know
for someone you do: sister's coworker, lover's friend
accountant's mother, your aunt's
high school rival.

7
black churches formed burial societies
after slavery. Every week you chipped
off a piece of your pay to save for the shovel
& the rough hands that would lower you.

I know some black folks now buying
their plot foot-by-foot. Saving for a
final mortgage.

8
it is día de los muertos & I have a check
folded in between the pages of a book about
genocide. I will send the money next week
to the other side of my family
& help bury grandma's sister.

9

I can't think of a black rapper who hasn't
contemplated their own death on record.
*Ready to die, life after death, death is certain,
do or die, get rich or die tryin', death certificate.*

This is natural.
All my verses mention
boxes or holes.

10

*once we lay this brother
down in the ground
we got work to do.*

*When I was a young boy
at the age of five
my mama said I gon' be
the greatest man alive.*

*These children don't
expect to live past 30.
They come to these funerals
& they represent.
They put themselves in
the place of the person
in the casket.*

CHAPTER 3

Unwavering Determination

For the boys and girls who grew in spite of these things to be man and woman, to laugh and dance and sing . . .

—Margaret Walker, *For My People*

Kevin Hopkins, 2022. Fabric, art, paint, vintage school desks. This image shows a life-size male student with a dated workbook in front of him.

POETIC REFLECTION

Lessons[1]

Jordan Stempleman

In one version of a country's history
the teacher's forehead empties out
as fog into owned open air.
But in another version
mothers are running their fingers across this
and that
the hollowed arcades from before we met
and after we eat
what we watch out for
and what could never be enough.
The cold quail.
The sparks that turn down bit by bit.
Wish now for all that can't consider be stirred.
For all that won't consider be stirred.
In all the strangers' faces
until there's the seen and the unseen.
And in all these names
that we memorize and replace
let them return to sounds that see again.
The once alien
decked out in the approximate togetherness
gone alike
in the wearing away.

The oral histories in the previous chapter illuminate the function and role of the Black female teachers in Hattiesburg, and the ways they developed places to promote education and a sense of autonomy. The way Mrs.

Jackson tutored children at a grocery store, in her home, or at church is an example of the dedication that existed. These sites of learning within the community were critical to student success and community uplift. William Sturkey asserts: "Schools, churches, and the homes of trusted community members were places of development and learning."[2] It is impossible to fully appreciate the oral histories without first considering the sense of autonomy participants maintained despite Jim Crow and the massive resistance to desegregation. The origins of how that sense of self and activism emerged is rooted in family, Black homes, and community. Mississippi and Hattiesburg are windows to our world—a microcosm of the failures of our country and the plight of the people refusing to accept the status quo, but making certain that we were aspiring and *becoming*.

Unlearning the Hush Begins at Home

Given the attempts to thwart desegregation, and the messages that Jim Crow segregation instilled about Black inferiority, how did Black women maintain agency and community? How did Black female educators successfully continue to teach? More importantly, how did they navigate becoming and remaining unhushed? Many of the answers are tied to Black homes and extended community. Stephen Berrey explains:

> The family unit extended into the community. [Patricia Hill] Collins describes a series of women-centered networks, including grandmothers, siblings, other relatives, neighbors, and even strangers, all of whom became what she calls the "othermothers" assisting the "blood mothers" (Collins, *Black Feminist Thought: Knowledge, Consciousness, and the Politics of Empowerment*, 173–99). This sharing of responsibilities strengthened communal bonds, and as Collins notes, it laid a foundation for activism within the community. Within the recollections of African Americans in rural Jim Crow Mississippi, one finds many of Collins's characteristics of black motherhood—and these "motherly" characteristics were not limited to women. As interviewees discuss their childhoods—who nurtured them, who taught them life lessons, who taught them how to act in Jim Crow society—they describe a network of individuals in the community, including both men and women. Grandparents, aunts and uncles, and neighbors were members of a family unit that helped children learn racial rules and unlearn ideologies of black inferiority.[3]

Agency and womanhood, as many participants mentioned, began early with messages in the home and from the community. Dr. Joyce Ladner discussed how her mother taught her children from a young age that they were as good as anyone else, to never be afraid to look a white person in their eyes, and to hold their head up.[4] Others described hearing similar messages that instilled a sense of empowerment, importance, and autonomy amid the confines of Jim Crow repressions. Stories and lessons in the home centered on family history, Black history, and the notion of excelling despite imposed barriers. Though it might be assumed that Black families lived only in fear, most families used history, protest, and discussions in the home to impart lessons and prepare children for the world. Research has detailed the role of the Black family and community regarding voice and activism. Berrey gives us an overview:

> Traditional archival records—state documents, mainstream or black newspapers, and personal papers—provide little or no detailed information about families and daily routines. While these sources are often understood as the most reliable records of the past, they can also be misleading. For example, in his study of race and media in 1960s Mississippi, media scholar Steven Classen searched the official paper documents for local black responses to local television coverage [*Resistance Begins at Home: The Black Family and Lessons in Survival and Subversion in Jim Crow Mississippi*] (2004, 140–45). He found no Black protest. Yet, as he spoke with local people he discovered an extensive record of protests of television from the Black community. As Classen's study demonstrates, for marginalized groups, oral histories can speak to the inherent silences of traditional archives (Michel-Rolph Trouillot, *Silencing the Past, Power, and the Production of History*, 1995).[5]

The silences in the archives conceal the ways that Black families and communities instilled a sense of agency into children as they grew up. These children were most impacted by the lessons they received at home, as those lessons counteracted the messages children growing up in the Jim Crow South received. Berrey expounds on this: "One might suspect that for children the initial recognition of blackness would have been tied to a lynching or some other dramatic event. However, of the hundreds of interviews I consulted for this study, none of the interviewees linked their initial racial awareness to an act of physical violence. Many children were unaware of the violence around them in part because their parents sheltered them."[6]

The efforts of parents, particularly mothers, in Black homes allowed children to not only navigate growing up during Jim Crow, but also to move beyond systemic and societal hindrances. They worked to instill a sense of racial and individual pride in children. Families in the Jim Crow era had conversations that ranged from explaining the realities of violence and the behavior necessary in certain spaces, to building the children's self-esteem and identity and teaching them to navigate the realities that came with the duality[7] of being Black and being a Black resident of Mississippi. This duality often meant navigating both racial oppression and the additional unwritten rules and landscape of the violence Black residents of Mississippi were subjected to. Parents worked to make their children aware of these truths while also reminding them that they were valued and equal in ability—they were as good as whites. Storytelling was used to pass down a sense of pride and history, and elders or grandparents helped reinforce this notion. As Patricia Hill Collins has noted, many of these lessons were led by the women in the home and community as a form of "resistance to oppression." The teachers and participants in this book followed those lessons from the women in their lives and transferred them to their classrooms. Collins refers to these interconnected groups as "nurturing networks," in that they helped connect children and youth to the community and societal issues.[8] This generational transferring of pro-Blackness and anti–hushed sentiments helped build resistance against the racist ideologies of second-class citizenship and produce educators and students who were able to see beyond the myth of inferiority.[9] Ultimately, the result was a generation that emerged prepared to use their voices and agency to dismantle Jim Crow, challenge inequities, and educate future generations to follow suit.[10]

Resistance in Mississippi to Compliance with *Brown*

In addition to navigating the Jim Crow South, Black female educators would be tasked with navigating the resistance that ensued after the 1954 Supreme Court ruling in *Brown v. Board of Education*. Many articles and documents were written opposing and showing resistance to the ruling. One such document implored the Supreme Court to reverse its decision for the betterment of mankind and the country. In "Segregation Is Constitutional but Compulsory Integration Is Unconstitutional," W. L. Easton, an attorney, stated:

> The pure Negros are necessarily hewers of wood and drawers of water. They have made no progress during their existence. Have they kept pace with the Caucasian race of Europe? Let historians run the parallel. A full-blooded Negro child can no more keep up with a white child than a possum can keep up with a fox. This is the ultimate test: Do you want your white daughter to marry a Negro man? Do you want her to return home after a few years with a brood of mulattos?[11]

This kind of rhetoric illustrates the mindset of much of the country, specifically in the South, and the kind of resistance that Black educators were facing. The abhorrent side of desegregation was that despite its intended goal of equality, it further exposed the racist thinking that existed. There was no chance for desegregation to be carried out in a fair or logical manner when this was the ideology undermining it from the start.

During the desegregation years from 1954 to 1970, many of these efforts to stave off integration and prevent Black educational success in Mississippi made Black female teachers rethink their decisions and careers.[12] Michael Fultz states, "As has been well established in the historiography of the immediate post-*Brown* years, southern massive resistance 'grew to full maturity' during the mid-to-late 1950s, in the aftermath of the May 1955 *Brown* II decision."[13] Even prior to *Brown*, segregationists and state officials attempted to increase funding to Black schools and increase teaching salaries, in the hopes of initially fending off integration. The thought was that if the school buildings were new and resources more abundant, integration would become a moot point. Schools such as Royal Street (later renamed Rowan) were renovated, and Earl Travillion was built. However, these new buildings and added funds did not create equality in any sense. William Sturkey attests that "building renovations and teacher-salary increases at black schools were always accompanied by better improvements at white schools. Black schools still received less financial support per pupil and sub-standard supplies. . . . The $11 million spent on black schools between 1946 and 1953 paled in comparison to the $30 million spent on white schools during that same period."[14]

State legislators privatized white public schools to stop desegregation efforts. Mississippi whites, resistant to desegregation and the civil rights movement, formed the White Citizens' Council and resorted to violence to upend desegregation efforts, and policies and practices were put into place to fire teachers who were involved with organizations seeking to disrupt this resistance. For example, if teachers were found to be members of the NAACP (National Association for the Advancement of Colored People) or the NACW (National Association of Colored Women), they could be fired on the spot. These forms of intimidation and bullying led to Black teacher displacement and dismissal.

These tactics were utilized throughout the South to hinder Black educators and ensure that the Black community's goals of racial uplift and educational success were thwarted. The ongoing, extensive trauma that Black teachers were exposed to particularly related to the uncertainty and loss of their economic livelihoods. Fultz expands on this idea: "For a period of approximately two decades, from the mid-1950s through the mid-1970s, African-American school staff at all levels—teachers, principals, coaches, counselors, band directors, even cafeteria workers—were fired, demoted, harassed, and bullied as White communities throughout the South reacted first to the prospect and then to the reality of court-ordered desegregation."[15] Fultz continues: "Dismissals, demotions, forced resignations, 'nonhiring,' token promotions, reduced salaries, diminished responsibility, coercion to teach subjects or grade levels other than those for which individuals were certified or had experience" were all tactics and practices used to displace Black educators.[16] Many Black educators went from working in insufficiently funded segregated Black schools to joblessness. Others went from being leaders in these segregated Black schools to being demoted and traumatized by their experiences in mandated desegregation experiments. Additionally, in the years following the *Brown* decision, many southern schools began to implement policies or manifestos that shared anti-desegregation sentiments, while some states threatened to withhold funding from states that desegregated. Among those caught in the crossfire of this changing landscape were Black female teachers in Mississippi, who, until recently, were essentially voiceless in the historical record.[17]

Throughout history, women have been formative in creating and shaping the stories passed down for generations. Redefining our history must include an accurate portrayal of the roles these women had in shaping pedagogy and community.[18] The accounts and recollections all attest to the commitment Black female educators made, reminding us that teachers faced seemingly insurmountable odds at times, yet they continued their careers to positively impact the lives of students, families, and communities.[19]

Protective Spaces

Homes and schoolhouses functioned as spaces that allowed participants in this book to move this tradition forward for their students. Patricia Hill Collins's research names places other than home that have historically functioned as protective spaces for Black women. She notes that Black women's relationships with one another, the role of mentoring and being mentored, and methods that use art, storytelling, music, and poetry all work toward providing protective spaces. All these elements were utilized in the pedagogy of Black women to create protective spaces in the schoolhouses. Curricula were tailored to not only meet the needs of students, but also crafted to motivate and inspire them. These elements were especially critical during Jim Crow.[20]

These spaces were beneficial to students and teachers, as they allowed Black women to feel empowered and assured. As Collins has discussed, "[t]hese spaces allowed Black women to resist the objectification as the

Other." Navigating the resistance to desegregation and functioning in white schools both would draw from the early lessons from home and the community. These spaces, both physical and psychological, that participants encountered throughout their upbringing would transfer into their teaching approaches.[21] Tenacity and fortitude allowed these women, and others, to find a way, even when it was bleak. As Dr. Ladner shared, "[m]uch of their resilience was forged in the throes of stark economic deprivation, which required them to keep functioning in the midst of

TABLE 2. Forrest County Public Schools and Hattiesburg Public Schools

Hattiesburg Public Schools ("City Schools"), desegregated in 1965	Forrest County Public Schools ("County Schools"), desegregated in 1970
Eaton (white school)	DePriest (Black school), closed in 1957
Walthall (white school)	Myers (Black school), closed in 1957
Woodley (white school)	Bay Springs (Black school), closed in 1957
Jefferson Davis (white school)	John White (Black school), closed in 1957
Grace Christian (white school)	Spring Field (Black school), closed in 1957
Thames (white school)	
Main Street (white school)	The above five schools were closed in 1957 and consolidated into one school—Earl Travillon Attendance Center. In 1970, when the county schools were desegregated, Travillon became a K–8 school, and high school students were forced to attend North Forrest, Petal, or Brooklyn (white schools).
Hattiesburg High School (white high school)	
Central Baptist School (private/white)	
Camp (Black school), closed	
Mary Bethune (Black school), closed	North Forrest (white high school), 1970
Grace Love (Black school), closed	Petal (white high school), 1970
W.H. Jones (Black school), closed	Brooklyn (white high school), 1970
Eureka (Black school), closed	
Royal Street (Black school), name later changed to Rowan and turned into an elementary school	Hattiesburg currently has two private schools, which are on average 89 percent white.
Lillie Burney (Black school), turned into an elementary school, and to date is a learning center	Mr. Cooper shared that there are approximately 82 counties in Mississippi, with a total of 132 superintendents in the state.

adversity. 'Been Down So Long, Seems Like Up to Me' is the title of an old Negro spiritual that speaks to this virtue. Being knocked down is nothing new to Black people."[22]

County Schools and City Schools

Desegregation occurred at different points in time in Hattiesburg based on whether the school was a city school or a county school. Despite all schools being in the same county of Forrest County, the city schools were classified as Hattiesburg Public Schools, while the county schools were classified as Forrest County Public Schools. At the time, the city had a higher population of white students, so desegregating in the city schools in 1965 was less threatening than it would have been to desegregate the county schools, with their higher populations of Black students. The county schools were forced to desegregate six years later, in 1970. The last class of seniors from Earl Travillion Attendance Center graduated in 1970.[23] Students who were seniors at Earl Travillion and were to graduate in May of 1971 ordered their caps and gowns, only to discover at the end of their winter break in December 1970 that their time at Travillion was over. In second semester (beginning January 1971), they were required to transfer to North Forrest, Petal, or Brooklyn High Schools.[24] This displacement occurred quickly, gave the students no prior warning, and disrupted their second semester of school by moving them from the Black schools they had known all their lives to white schools. Out of all the Black schools, to date only two remain (Earl Travillion and Rowan). The chart below overviews schools in both Hattiesburg Public Schools and Forrest County Public Schools. It offers a sense of school closures that occurred after desegregation (as Black schools would close), and lists the schools that participants reference in their oral histories.

HISTORICAL VIGNETTE
Christopher M. Span

Twice Saving Democracy in America

Black people have played a pivotal role in safeguarding democracy in America not once, but twice. The significance of this narrative is profound, especially when considering the transformative impact of landmark events such as *Brown v. Board of Education* and its aftermath.

In reflecting on the journey toward democracy, it becomes apparent that the foundational principles of American democracy were initially exclusive, catering only to a select few. Democracy, as originally conceived, favored landowning, white, Christian, and male individuals, leaving marginalized communities, including African Americans, on the periphery.

Yet, even amid the shackles of slavery, African Americans held on to the ideals of democracy, believing in its promise and potential for all. The first instance of Black people saving democracy occurred with the election of Abraham Lincoln, which triggered the secession of the slave South and ignited the Civil War. In response, enslaved individuals seized the opportunity to undermine the institution of slavery, whether through acts of resistance, espionage, or even joining the Union Army as soldiers.

The second instance in this saga unfolded with the landmark decision in *Brown v. Board of Education*, which challenged the legality of segregation in public schools. However, it was the subsequent civil rights movement that breathed life into the aspirations of *Brown*, energizing communities to push for meaningful change.

In Mississippi, a bastion of resistance to desegregation, the story continued. Sixteen years after *Brown*, the teachers of Hattiesburg emerged as catalysts for change, advocating for compliance with the law and challenging systemic injustices. Their tireless efforts epitomized the resilience and determination of African Americans in the fight for equality.

Thus, the narrative of Black people twice saving America extends beyond historical events—it encompasses the everyday struggles and triumphs of individuals committed to realizing the democratic ideals upon which the nation was founded. In understanding the role of *Brown* and its impact on communities like Hattiesburg, we gain insight into the ongoing quest for justice and empowerment, illuminating an American history defined by resilience, courage, and unwavering determination.

Rebecca Marimutu, *Contact #13*, 2021. Archival pigment print.

POETIC REFLECTION

Miss Banks[25]

Maxine Chernoff

Missy was speechless
when Miss Banks arrived
and said she was the new teacher. Missy asked Crystal
how it could be that Nasty Miss Elmer, hair red as a barn, had left to get
married. Good riddance the girls agreed and
"Who would marry her?"

"A teacher like us!
Look at her hair!" Sally pointed to the beautiful
'fro Miss Banks allowed
to flank her face.

"My mom makes me wear these," Sally added, tugging at her braids, "but I have an idea. We'll wear our hair the same!"

"Let's Be Miss Banks!"
Gerald shouted. The girls laughed. "You're no girl, Gerald."
To which Gerald replied: "Miss Banks a girl? She's a lady, for sure. Look at that dress!" He made a whistle.

". . . She's just like us," he added. The girls laughed and showed up the very next day with their new hairdos and ruffly Sunday dresses because it was a holiday of sorts.

And all year, even when Miss Banks lost her temper and made a sound under her breath, the class could not stop smiling. Someday they'd all be teachers like Miss Banks. Whatever she said was right by them.

CHAPTER 4

Love Is Resistance

> Those who love us never leave us alone with our grief.
> At the moment they show us our wound, they reveal they have the medicine.
> —Zora Neale Hurston, *Barracoon: The Story of the Last "Black Cargo"*

Kevin Hopkins, Community art piece at HAW Contemporary Gallery, Unlearning the Hush exhibition, curated by Marlee Bunch and Kevin Hopkins, 2022. Chalk on chalkboard. Attendees of the exhibit were invited to draw and interact with the art piece, making it a community piece that represented many voices.

POETIC REFLECTION

Haint Blue[1]
Cole Swensen

On the frame around the porch where its edges or ashes or an
    eyelash
of feathering porchlight quietly annihilates darkness all
    throughout Georgia
the frames are painted this particular shade because it keeps
    the ghosts away or
keeps them closer, curled up in the home I can't remember
    which one was first
to point out the robin's egg laid on the third storey windowsill
    on the inside
a bird born within the house of such a deep blue that we've
    never been able to find it.

Themes

As young Joyce Ladner walked home from elementary school, she was greeted by elders in the neighborhood who stopped her and asked to see her grades. The older women knew it was report card day, and they were sure to be standing outside, inquiring about how students in the neighborhood were doing in their classes. They gifted her a dime for each A she had made and told her that she would be somebody when she grew up. This left a lasting impression. Love is an act of resistance, an act of healing, and acts such as this worked to encourage and support students. Ladner tells us:

> Children in traditional communities discovered sooner or later that their lives mattered to a lot people whom they barely knew and to whom they were not directly accountable. . . . It didn't matter that I was someone else's daughter. I never forgot those dimes. To me, they symbolized the faith these women had in me and the strength of their belief in what I could do with my life.[2]

Despite having to navigate difficult aspects of teaching, participants' stories made it clear that education was more than a career. It was a way of affirming students, bringing with it the hope of bettering society. These educators were considering every aspect of the classroom while preparing their students to enter a racialized and unjust society. Themes that emerged during the research for the interviews in this book included

1. the importance of Black spaces;
2. the Black community as the counternarrative;
3. mentors and kinship;
4. creative innovation and the whole child; and
5. empowering Black identity.

Teachers as a Collective

Research by Vanessa Siddle Walker and others offers context to the research for this book regarding the positive characteristics and benefits of Black female educators. An overlooked but essential aspect of understanding this history is what Siddle Walker details regarding the way that Black educators worked collectively to enact change. This collective approach allowed educators to not only create associations and teacher study groups, but to align their beliefs and goals regarding what would best support Black students. It was through this collective organizing that they successfully navigated the system, by discovering not only what students needed, but how to implement it. Siddle Walker states, "Usually products of Southern segregated schools themselves, these teachers both implicitly identified with student needs and aspirations and, simultaneously, understood how to negotiate the world beyond the local community. Having lived the benefit of education, the teachers could also tell students how to move beyond the limited life possibilities of a segregated world and how to use education to achieve a middleclass life."[3] The women of Hattiesburg went to great lengths to keep up their teaching credentials and their own education so that they could be effective and prepared to best teach their students and families.[4] Educator and principal Mrs. Eleanor Deloris Goins recounted the ways in which she and her sister had to secure their own education: "I lived in walking distance of William Carey College, but since Blacks were not allowed to attend, I had to go elsewhere. Teachers often used their summers to travel to colleges outside of Mississippi to take courses that would allow them to finish their degrees. Most of the teachers I taught with had their master's degree, which proves how seriously we took education."[5] Education was so valued that Black educators traveled, spent summers away, and navigated segregated colleges to ensure they perfected their craft and continued their own learning.

Vanessa Siddle Walker reminds us:

> In espousing the philosophies they [Black educators] held, they both recreated themselves in their students and made possible the continued advancement of a people with whom they identified. Through their education and continuous pursuit of additional education, the teachers demonstrated their own desire to be better than what was expected of White teachers. Just as important, when they told African American children they could "be somebody," they in effect were examples of the truths they espoused, thus making themselves significant role models.[6]

One constant at the core of Hattiesburg's Black education and Black experiences has been Black educators and mentors. Hattiesburg teachers worked to shape and mold themselves and their students so excellence could emerge. Out of thirty-four teachers at Earl Travillion in 1962, twenty-five were women. All the teachers had bachelor's degrees, and four had master's degrees—showing the level of commitment to personal growth and self-education. These attributes and the content knowledge these educators obtained helped raise their classrooms beyond the boundaries of everyday southern life.

William Sturkey elaborates on this: "There was never a time in Southern history when black people were not active. From organizing through churches and pouring resources into black schools, African Americans had always gotten together within their communities to help improve the lives and prospects of their fellow black citizens."[7] These efforts allowed teachers to expand their reach and expertise, ultimately enriching classroom spaces. Today, with fewer Black and Brown educators, we see the detrimental impact on our communities and students when there are no windows and mirrors through which students and communities can see themselves—which is yet another reason to excavate and illuminate these histories.[8]

The Importance of Black Spaces

Participants all spoke about the importance of Black spaces, and the loss that occurred when they were disrupted. And though Black schools and spaces often lacked resources, participants shared that this deficit was countered with the sense of community that permeated these spaces.

Educator and scholar Jarvis Givens wants everyone to understand that within Black schools and communities a true commitment to the development of Black students existed:

Black teachers reimagined what constituted knowledge: who could be producers and repositories of knowledge; and, ultimately, how students were to conceive of human life and their place within it. Generation after generation of Black teachers arrived at this conclusion, compelling them to build on liberatory curricular visions that can be traced from the antebellum era through the twentieth century.[9]

Black spaces were a respite from the violence and tension that was everywhere in Mississippi during this time, and educators used curriculum and their relationships with students to reinforce and celebrate Blackness.[10] Participants shared that the removal of these spaces post-*Brown* was a detriment to Black teachers and students. This fact was made evident after desegregation, when Black students and teachers were now required to function in a white space.[11] Moving to white spaces meant that Black female educators had to overperform and bear their Blackness as a deficit, rather than the benefit it had previously been in Black schools.[12] Tia Madkins notes that "[n]early 39,000 Black teachers in 17 states lost their jobs from 1954 to 1965. Subsequently, the Black teachers who maintained employment with these districts experienced internal resegregation. These teachers were given the task of educating only Black students while their White colleagues taught White students at so-called integrated school sites. The percentage of Blacks in the teaching workforce began to decline such that by 1978, Blacks comprised only 12% of the national workforce and [this] has steadily declined over time to only 8% currently."[13] Additionally, the Department of Education discontinued tracking school statistics for students and staff by race after 1954, making the statistics we have regarding employment data likely erroneous. Samuel Ethridge states, "It became almost impossible to find out comparative official racial employment figures between 1954–1964."[14]

As educator and principal Mrs. Woullard described it, this loss of Black educators meant that not only were educators negatively impacted, but also that achievement was viewed differently for Black students after desegregation. She explained that Black teachers saw unlimited potential in students, but white teachers often failed to recognize their abilities. She said, "I have a sorority sister who started out at USM (University of Southern Mississippi), and the teacher told her not to even think about being a lawyer. Oh, yes. And she defied him, because today she is a judge here in Hattiesburg."[15] Black spaces offered a sense of hope. Bearing witness to this success in the Jim Crow South meant something, as Vanessa Siddle Walker reminds us: "it was a testimony to the fact that school and learning led to personal advancement and possibilities." Siddle Walker's research offers an in-depth analysis of books and conference papers that examine segregated schools. This research allowed her to identify recurring themes missing from previous studies, and concluded that factors such as positive relationships, high expectations, and affirmation of students created an environment in which students thrived, despite the lack of resources.[16] These assets have been reported in subsequent studies as well (e.g., Morris and Morris, among others).[17] These factors created spaces that allowed for the advancement and affirmation of Black students.[18]

Participants shared their own memories of growing up in Black spaces because of segregation, and the positive effects that brought. They also spoke about the shift they witnessed as educators when they watched Black students displaced and mistreated in the newly desegregated white spaces compared to their experiences in Black spaces, as has been documented elsewhere.[19] What was the cost of losing schools that were all-Black spaces? What was the cost of seeing the names of the schools stripped, most of the buildings torn down, and the Black educators who had taught them their entire lives now in peril of losing their jobs? More importantly, what would happen when Black students who were accustomed to the high expectations of their Black teachers were forced into classrooms with white teachers who often viewed Black students as inferior? Desegregation would prove how important these all-Black spaces were.

Mrs. Goins shared her own stories of growing up as a student in all-Black classrooms and said that she "had phenomenal teachers who made her more curious about learning."[20] She said her teachers made sure that she learned Black history, that she was disciplined, and that she always did her best. She was able to see herself in them.

The Black spaces in these classrooms had the makings of what we know today as culturally responsive classrooms: high expectations, dedicated teachers, and an insular community that worked to eradicate the messages being sent from living in the Jim Crow South.

The interactions observed between white teachers and Black students indicate the disruption and differences that took place after Black spaces were dismantled—racism seeping into the classroom and creating doubts about ability and intelligence. Mrs. Bobbitt, special education educator, observed:

> I tell you what I have seen when I worked alongside of white educators. They didn't necessarily teach our children. They didn't necessarily teach Black kids. And you know, I kinda wrestled with that same thing with my own children when I was deciding where they were going to go to school. Because I had seen it, I mean, I even saw it when I was at the high school. Some of the white teachers just didn't teach the Black kids. You just got by if you did not put yourself out there. Okay. But you

could've been a better student.... It's called Pygmalion in the classroom. It's like I'll set a level for you, you know, I'm here and you are there. And so it's like they don't have the time for your questions.[21]

Lonnie Bunch reinforced the importance of Black spaces and how history and museums can help create and preserve these sacred spaces today:

> It is really important to recognize that there is a profound need for Black spaces. It's profound on several levels. On one hand, one of the challenges of desegregation was that you move away from Black spaces, right? That sort of integration became the promised land. So, rather than go to the Joe store that you've gone to for 20 years, you go elsewhere, because you can now do it. I think that what we really need to recognize is that without those spaces, you lose the opportunity to be yourself. You lose the opportunity to be shaped by a community. You lose the opportunity of saying, I need help and this space helped me do what I need to do.
>
> That's why it's important for me to build museums. It's important to also create conceptual spaces, whether it's through oral histories, or whatever. So that you have an opportunity. There always is a "Black Reservoir" to dip into.[22]

Black spaces were (and are) fundamental in ensuring students were encouraged to move beyond the invisible and visible barriers that existed.

The Counternarrative Is the Black Community

It would be difficult to discuss the oral histories presented in this book without illustrating the inextricable connection between the participants and the community. Dr. Christopher M. Span speaks about this sense of education among the first freed slaves: "To be educated was to be respected; to be educated was to be a citizen. Accordingly, countless black Mississippians willingly sought out schooling, viewing it as the foundation for self-improvement and one means for attaining social and economic parity in slavery's aftermath."[23] Knowing this background and data about Mississippi, and the way in which freedpeople regarded learning, helps to give us a rich background to understand the great sense of community and pride that had been built in Black people long before the battle of *Brown v. Board of Education*.

Prior to *Brown*, Black education and the Black community were synonymous because of segregation by law. The great triad of church, community, and Black educators worked to ensure that Black students both were successful and had their needs wholly met. Participants all mentioned the sense of community that existed, particularly prior to desegregation.[24] H. Richard Milner and Tyrone C. Howard state:

> Irvine and Irvine, in their examination of many Black communities post-*Brown* ["The Impact of the Desegregation Process on the Education of Black Students: A Retrospective Analysis"], described the school desegregation process as iatrogenesis, a medical concept which means that the intervention which was used to supposedly cure or heal a particular ailment turns out to have a more detrimental impact than the initial problem. In short, they argued that a comprehensive analysis of the *Brown* ruling cannot be merely limited to the condition of schooling for Black students but must also entail the deterioration of many Black communities as a result of school closings[, p]articularly in light of the fact that Black schools, along with Black churches, were frequently considered to be hubs or center points of their respective communities. Black teachers had their skin complexion examined, were demoted, and [experienced] loss of voice after the *Brown* decision. Prior to the decision, the teachers had meaningful influences in what happened in the schools and how Black students were educated. Moreover, the community held Black teachers in high regard.[25]

When asked about her experience growing up in an all-Black community, Mrs. Bobbitt answered:

> That community piece is so key. It's so important. When I was growing up, you saw that community piece—our teachers lived in our neighborhoods or they went to our churches. They knew our parents and our cousins. If you lost a family member, they grieved right along with you, you know? I guess a lot depends on the community that you live in. I loved where we lived. Teachers lived in the community where I lived. Some of them went to the same church with me. We had a black dentist who didn't live too far from us. I think they just set the standards for us.[26]

The beauty of the Black community was the mirror that it created for young Black children and students, letting them see themselves in the professionals around them—dentists, teachers, and bankers. Mr. Charles Cooper, who was both a student and an educator, reflected on the thriving Black-owned businesses that lined Mobile Street in Hattiesburg when he was growing up, and the pride it instilled. He spoke about the differences evident in Hattiesburg from the past to the present, to provide context for the events that took place in Mississippi in the 1960s:

> Mobile Street and Palmers Crossing are now ghost towns. There is nothing there anymore.... It's sad. It's pitiful. Those areas were once thriving parts of Hattiesburg's history. When I was young, we didn't have to go to

McDonald's, we had everything we needed in the community—a burger joint, movie theater, everything.

When I went to school, I loved being there and I didn't want to leave. Our schools in Hattiesburg are often misrepresented. I did not attend Freedom Schools, because my family and community felt as though I was receiving a good education. Freedom Schools might have been needed in many parts of Mississippi, but I would say that Hattiesburg was not one of them. We had teachers fully capable of teaching us, and they had been doing it for years.

I grew up considering myself an activist. My senior year, I got involved in SNCC and helped canvass for voting. Many of the residents had no idea what SNCC was, so we helped to tell them about it and their right to vote. It was dangerous, but we were all so convinced that we needed to help fight this fight. If we had to die, we would die. It's so sad today that our history is not talked about enough. . . . Just think of a five-block street with nothing but Black businesses lining both sides. On the corner they had an old newsstand, everybody knew about it, and the church. The newsstand and church are still there, but those are the only buildings on that street right now. What it looked like in the 1960s is just a memory. It is not the place it used to be. People do not have a clue about integration. The good was that we [the Black community] were together, the bad was that we were segregated, and nothing was created equal, and it was not what democracy was intended to be. All we needed and wanted was the right to go in the front door instead of being forced to go through the back door. After desegregation, many teachers and families left. When jobs were lost, the Black community could not sustain businesses.[27]

The memories Mr. Cooper speaks of were echoed by most participants—a happy childhood, good education, and engaged community. The intersection of the community and the work of the educators were intertwined—a commitment to the whole child. I think of Zola Jackson again, and the stories I have heard about her, a woman who was never afraid to disrupt the system or the status quo. She was always willing to share what she had to benefit someone else, whether that meant taking books from her own home to give to a student, visiting a student at home, tutoring a student that needed extra support, or even making ice cream to share with her neighbors. That is the crux of community.

A single teacher in the Black community had the ability to impact so many, and would often teach three to four generations of one family.[28] The community had ties that spanned generations. Teachers and families lived and functioned side by side, and the resulting proximity, collaboration, and relationships improved the lives of students and children in the community. As Mrs. Bobbitt shared, "Everyone worked toward the common goal of enriching the community."[29] Mrs. Armstrong, who grew up with Mrs. Jackson, echoed Bobbitt's sentiments and described life in a segregated community as being like the folk story Stone Soup—everyone brought something to put in the pot, and eventually there was enough for all. The sense of kinship and community was an ever-present shield that protected Black folks from some of the daily concerns of racial unrest in the South. Mrs. Armstrong recounted:

> Our community lived by the phrase it takes a village. Despite some struggles our community had with young people having to choose work over school and some struggles with lack of literacy, education was viewed as valuable. The elders helped young folks avoid mistakes and when a neighbor was in need, you helped. There was cohesiveness established in schools and neighborhoods. Our community was solid. You had the churches, schools, and the community all interwoven, and everyone looked out for each other. There was a great sense of connection.[30]

Recollections of how the Black community thrived prior to *Brown* served not only as a testament to Black abilities, but also was the counternarrative to the demeaning messages sent by white society in the Jim Crow South.[31]

Mentors and Kinship

Black educators have historically advocated for students and understood the importance and power of collaboration.[32] And while Black teachers may not have been able to provide access to the resources found in white schools, they were able to help students have pride in who they were, which allowed for a confidence and sense of worth that propelled students to do great things. Dr. Joyce Ladner's life illustrates this; she went on to become a leader in the civil rights movement who helped to plan Freedom Summer and the March on Washington, a first-generation college student who obtained her PhD, the first interim Black female at Howard University, and more. Mentors such as Mrs. Jackson, the Dahmer family, and Clyde Kennard would all be formative in helping support and inspire Ladner's aspirations. One of the ways educators and community members were able to instill this sense of worth in students was through the relationships that they built as mentors and extended family. Educators and community members worked in tandem to help ensure that Black students felt assured and had people who were sincerely invested in their future. Together, students benefited and teachers and families thrived.

Mrs. Armstrong shared her sentiments about the exceptional teachers she had. When asked about her perspective as a student growing up with all-Black female teachers, she answered, "We had excellent teachers. They were caring and wanted you to learn beyond the basics and beyond the classroom. I had mostly female teachers growing up. They had high expectations and were part of our village."[33] Because Black teachers were formative in the community, many worked to assure that students received a quality education and had the guidance of a mentor. Teachers stepped easily into these roles to help create a meaningful educational experience for Black students in a system that has been historically unequal. As far back as 1870, the educational system failed to include Black folks as part of the equation. Though education was supposed to be the "great equalizer," it was not. If the state of Mississippi and the citizens creating the resistance against an equal education for Black students would not ensure that Black students received a fair and just education, then Black teachers would work to counterbalance these ideological and structural deficits.

The educational historian Vanessa Siddle Walker recognized this truth. In her estimation of the importance of Black teachers during segregation, Siddle Walker explained, "[C]onsistently remembered for their high expectations for student success, for their dedication, and for their demanding teaching style, these [Black] teachers appear to have worked with the assumption that their job was to be certain that children learned the material presented."[34] Jon Hale continues this notion: "Black educators inextricably linked their professional labor to protecting and then expanding a right to an education as the courts institutionalized de jure segregation throughout the South, particularly after the *Plessy v. Ferguson* (1896) decision justified a racist, segregated, and unequal system of education. As the contradictions of segregation increasingly infringed upon the constitutional right to an education at the state level, Black educators organized professional associations to defend their right to an education during the Jim Crow era by professionalizing their craft and implementing progressive instruction in the classroom."[35] Mrs. Armstrong witnessed this through the mentoring and pedagogy that her teachers offered. She shared what made her teachers exceptional: "They were always trying to educate the whole child with learning that reached beyond just books. Our teachers understood that learning was about life and book learning. Their teaching naturally incorporated both."[36] The combination of progressive teaching and high expectations resulted in an approach that ensured students' academic and socioemotional needs were met. This commitment to students left a lasting impression.

Nurturing the Whole Child

The unequal resources and lack of access to classroom materials that Black teachers faced prior to desegregation has been well documented and cited by researchers. It has also been acknowledged that Black educators have historically been remembered for supporting Black students, having high expectations, and maintaining a structured and orderly classroom. Teachers worked to educate the whole child by attending to both their academic and social needs. What has not been largely documented is the fact that Black teachers found ways to make sure that lack of resources did not prevent students from learning, as they used curriculum and collaboration as a means toward equitable outcomes. The celebrations and joys embedded within these educator's stories also has not been largely documented. What these women had in abundance was innovation, creativity, empathy, and the ability to use these skills to help counter some of the deficits they faced. To give an example, my grandmother, Mrs. Jackson, used her own funds to help create a library in her classroom and for the school. Mrs. Goins would help lead a school focused on gifted and talented students. When there were no workbooks for students, teachers created them. When the lack of resources meant there was no yearbook for the students, teachers gathered pictures and helped create annuals for them. Stories like these emerged throughout the interviews and were common.

Mrs. Armstrong recalled the ways her mother, who was a teacher, also shared informal lessons with her and other students:

> We attended the Black school, so all our books were tattered and torn, backs torn off them by the white kids who'd used them, pages raggedy, and these were the books that we had to learn from and Black teachers had to teach from. My sister and one of her friends were complaining because the books were torn up, and my mother had told them the story about how it's not what's on the outside of the book—so what if it doesn't have a back. It's what's inside the books. This is what we're trying to teach you and this is what you need to learn. If you could look inside the book and read, and know what was in there, that is what matters. Lessons were always embedded in what was spoken at home.[37]

These lessons helped empower Black identity and shape a whole child approach that was rooted in pedagogical methods that extended beyond the books, as teachers met the needs of the whole child by imparting life lessons, using teaching practices that were directed to academic and social needs, and finding ways to make learning enjoyable.

The insight from participants offers examples of the ways in which Black female teachers navigated the circumstances of the time. These teachers were using culturally responsive teaching before it had a name, and were embodying trauma-informed care and social-emotional learning in their classrooms before the terms were known or used as they are today. For example, when educators taught about Black history and important historical or current figures, they were allowing students to see themselves as capable. When they were tutoring before or after school, they were offering individualized and differentiated learning and support. As they reminded students to wash their hands and look presentable, they were attending to social development. Finally, as they were sharing information about being civically engaged, they were offering opportunities for students to consider societal concerns and real-world issues, and teaching students how to navigate both.

Mrs. Goins described the teachers' goals: "We wanted to make sure our families knew how to do what was best for their children, and not get pushed into situations once integration happened. We were not afraid to advocate and use our voices whether it was quietly or loudly for our students."[38] The teachers' efforts did not go unnoticed by students and families. Visiting homes, teaching about self-care (e.g., personal hygiene), and exploring Black history were commonplace practices in Hattiesburg classrooms.

Siddle Walker continues this sentiment: "Teachers held extracurricular tutoring sessions, visited homes and churches in the community where they taught, even when they did not live in the community, and provided guidance about 'life' responsibilities. They talked with students before and after class, carried a student home if it meant the child would be able to participate in some extracurricular activity he or she could not otherwise participate in, purchased school supplies for their classrooms, and helped to supply clothing for students whose parents had fewer financial resources."[39] This kind of devotion is further supported by the information shared by participants—these educators went far beyond the basic expectations of teaching.

Mrs. Fowler, an educator for forty-four years, reported that working with children on all aspects of growth was her primary concern as a teacher. Respect, learning, and teaching students how to function on a day-to-day basis were aspects of her pedagogy and classroom methods. "Black teachers would do anything to make sure that the children were taken care of in the classroom, because we knew what they were up against once they left us. Before desegregation, Black students knew exactly what to expect in the classroom."[40]

Mutual respect, high expectations, and learning that fostered a positive self-identity were foundational parts of these classrooms. Mrs. Hale-Green reflected on how her role as a school counselor allowed her to see how teachers went above and beyond to make certain that a high level of learning was taking place: "Black teachers had little to no resources, yet they make sure that everyone learned. The teachers I had truly cared. They were invested in their students and their own continued learning. They wanted to make sure that students learned and could contribute to the world." She said that it was something she witnessed consistently and time and time again from Black educators.[41]

These reflections and histories offer explanations as to why Black female educators were so successful in nurturing well-educated and confident students despite segregation, a success that stemmed from the classroom experience being cultivated by these dedicated teachers.

Empowering Black Identity

One of the most empowering narratives that emerged from these oral histories was the focus the educators had on making certain that their students had a strong sense of self and a positive racial identity. Understanding the benefits that Black educators bring to students of color regarding identity development, self-confidence, and pride helps to illuminate the generational and long-term impact that *not* having these elements in desegregated schools has had on our students of color historically and today.

Mrs. Manning spoke about how teaching helped to foster a sense of pride in students: "Children need to see they are loved and supported, and I was proud to have played a role in helping to build self-esteem and a sense of self in the children."[42] Mrs. Hale-Green shared similar sentiments: "Black women took on an active role to try to make Black students always feel accepted in the schools and elsewhere. Their concern for education did so much for students and the Black community."[43] Vanessa Siddle Walker's research references the strong education that Black teachers and the community helped cultivate: "The community supported the school financially, the administrators were highly professional, the school climate emphasized both institutional and interpersonal caring as well as attending to the state curriculum, and the teachers were strong advocates for their students."[44] This focus on interpersonal caring resulted in students who understood their potential in learning and beyond.

Mrs. Goins's choice to become an educator was influenced by the positive experiences she had growing up with all-Black teachers:

> I chose to become a teacher because I had great teachers growing up in Hattiesburg. Teachers like Mrs. Heath and Mrs. Jackson were the reasons I wanted to be a teacher. Black women knew how to teach and reach Black students. Black teachers brought tolerance and patience to the classroom. They had great discipline and curiosity. They would make learning enjoyable and engaging for students, and they emphasized the importance of reading. They didn't take no for an answer and held you to high expectations.[45]

The sentiments of participants paint a picture of what Siddle Walker describes as the "three A's (advocacy, aspiration, access)," clearly demonstrating that Black educators were proficient in adequately providing for Black students:

> Long before the *Brown* decision, Black educators had achieved two of those three goals. With organizations like the Educators Association (EA), they had created powerful platforms for advocacy, and thanks in large part to that organizational structure, they had created a large network of schools that cared for Black children and supported their aspirations for full citizenship. The whole idea was to prepare them for a world that didn't exist yet, by teaching them not just to master academic content but also to use the tools of democracy—logic, persuasion, oratory.... So the hope was that integration would allow them to add the third A to the first two. In addition to the advocacy and aspiration they had already created, they would also get access to all of the resources, equipment, ideas, and opportunities that had been denied to them. But in reality, when they got the third A, they lost the other two. That's the "compromise" that allowed the country to preserve the language of desegregation while creating policies that diminished the hopes of Black educators for a fair desegregation.[46]

The hope of desegregation rested on the idea that it would provide Black students with access to a fair and equal educational experience. However, as Siddle Walker has shown, this is not what occurred. While the Black community had previously helped provide advocacy and aspiration, after desegregation this fractured, leaving the community and students in a vulnerable and perilous state. Dr. Joyce Ladner's book *The Ties That Bind* looks closely at the importance of the Black community as it existed during segregation, specifically regarding the formation of Black identity. Ladner asserts:

> Segregation, at times so burdensome for adults, fortified children in many ways. In our churches, schools, and strictly segregated neighborhoods, our African American teachers, preachers, and other caring adults talked often about dignity, carried themselves in a dignified

manner, and treated us with respect. A positive group identity therefore developed within the confines of our insular environments. Just as it has been proved that female students in all-girls schools develop a greater capacity for success than do girls in coeducational schools, so did we have greater opportunities for building a positive identity among ourselves in the absence of confusing, inconsistent messages about our abilities. Most African American adults of my generation shared similar experiences. In the main, we knew who we were at a very early age.[47]

All participants spoke to the sense of identity they felt and drew connections to how community, respect, and love helped nurture and affirm this. They emphasized that the community was foundational to providing a sense of consistency—if you needed food, someone would share from their garden or pantry; if you needed toys or clothing for your child, someone at church would help. Teachers were at the center of helping to make certain that students felt supported and proud of who they were. This was a cornerstone of their success—loving as an act of resistance.

HISTORICAL VIGNETTE
Christopher M. Span

Love Is Resistance

"Love is resistance." This profound statement encapsulates a truth that resonates deeply, for there are few forces as potent in challenging the established order as the act of nurturing individuals who have historically been marginalized, fostering in them the confidence and competence to defy societal expectations. Throughout American history, this dynamic has been exemplified time and again.

Consider the indispensable role of mentors like Charles Hamilton Houston in shaping the trajectory of Thurgood Marshall's career. Houston, the visionary architect behind legal strategies that dismantled segregation, cultivated a cadre of talented lawyers across racial lines. Marshall, under Houston's guidance, would lead groundbreaking cases such as *Brown v. Board of Education*, symbolizing the enduring impact of mentorship in effecting monumental change.

Personal experiences underscore the transformative power of mentorship. The profound impact of being mentored by someone who not only understands but respects one's strengths and vulnerabilities cannot be overstated. It fosters a sense of being valued and empowered to strive for one's best self, even amid the inherent fragility of such relationships.

The enduring love for community and commitment to resistance are evident in the stories of teachers navigating the challenges of Jim Crow Mississippi. Despite facing systemic barriers, they remained steadfast in their dedication to nurturing future generations and advocating for change. Theirs is a testament to the resilience and determination inherent in the pursuit of justice and equity.

At its core, the intertwining of love and resistance embodies a profound truth—that true progress often emerges from the tension between the desire for change and the forces seeking to maintain the status quo. Through mentorship and advocacy, the teachers of Jim Crow Mississippi exemplify a commitment to realizing a more just and equitable society, transcending barriers of race and circumstance.

In exploring these themes, we illuminate the enduring legacy of mentorship and advocacy, affirming the pivotal role of teachers as agents of change within their communities. Theirs is a narrative of resilience, empowerment, and unwavering dedication to shaping a brighter future for generations to come.

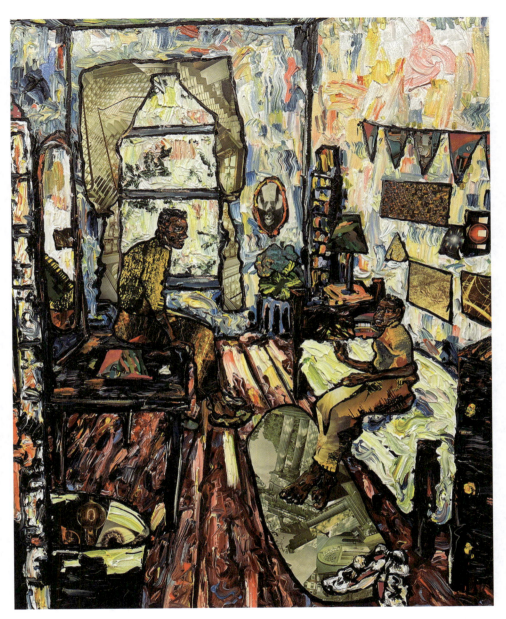

Mario Joyce, *All Your Selfish Ways*, 2023. Photographed by Christian Nguyen. Courtesy of UTA Artist Space and Mario Joyce. "This painting is a conversation between two young Black men in an academic setting about how different their backgrounds are from one another, both personally and ancestrally. It is speaking about how Blackness is not a monolith."

POETIC REFLECTION

Annihilation No. 7–11[48]

Stanley E. Banks

(For Pappa Dad)

His grandmother rolled
the dice for him
when she put her money
where her heart was.
She bet that she could
change the destiny of
an at-risk child who
wet the bed until he
was in the fifth grade
and talked to nine teddy
bears to get inspiration.
While his battering father,
jitterbug uncle and
their drinking buddies
bet that he would join
them on their favorite
corner to turn up a shared bottle,
his grandmother insisted that
he would be and do better—
but *he* didn't even believe
that at the time.
On a defining night after
his seventeenth birthday
with the bet on the line,
he gripped his father's
neck in a murderous clutch

and would have killed him
(his grandmother's son),
but in that instant
he heard her soft plea;
she called in her marker,
and when her grandson
released his pain,
her gamble for his
life paid off twice.

CHAPTER 5

Legacies and Artifacts

It is not unusual to sift through ashes
and find an unburnt picture.
—Nikki Giovanni, "The Women Gather"

Kevin Hopkins, *Mentors*, 2022. This image features Lonnie Bunch, Joyce Ladner, Christopher M. Span, and Linda Armstrong. The image represents the mentors in our lives who help shape and guide us.

POETIC REFLECTION

African American Literature I[1]
Ashley M. Jones

for VWS

she's crazy / they said / she's so crazy and you don't learn anything

    richard wright alice walker frantz fanon ralph ellison—nothings in disguise as somethings

look at her hair / look how it sticks out / look how she dresses/ look look look

    what did I see but myself in her? fro picked out and loud, fabrics draped like regal rags

she's too old to teach us / she's senile / she doesn't know what she's doing

    in this world, even the phd doesn't equal proficiency—black modifies scholar

why do we even have to take this class? / I'd rather take shakespeare / milton / someone important

    I exist I exist I exist I exist even though the universe says *no* in iambic pentameter

I said:

I said:

finally, I said: I am learning / she is brilliant / just learn, stop resisting / these books these stories are   mine

you only get A's because you're black / you only get A's because you're black

    in this world, even an honors designation doesn't equal proficiency / black modifies student

sometimes   even   I   doubted   you

who was I to say you were wrong, who were any of us?

didn't we see that the gleam in your eye was not eccentricity, senility, but the very last drop /

of your hope?

CHAPTER 5

Student Perspectives

Mr. Charles Cooper's oral history photo (shown in chapter 2) is from the beginning days of his teaching career. He is standing in front of a chalkboard, his handwriting neat on the board behind him and his countenance full of pride. At the time the photo was taken, Mr. Cooper would not yet know the many students he would impact, bringing the lessons he had learned from his teachers into his own classroom, and forging generational legacies. These lessons and teaching approaches would impact *all* of his students, including a young white male student (Don) who would go home each day sharing stories about Mr. Cooper with his family. Don's father (Ed) would request to meet with Mr. Cooper, wanting to learn more about the teacher his son spoke about daily. The two would forge a long relationship.

Inspired by his teachers and mentors, specifically Mr. Fowler and Mr. Harris, Mr. Cooper knew the impact that teaching could have. When he was growing up, Mr. Cooper felt as though he could be anything, thanks to the affirmations and guidance of his teachers.

Every participant interviewed for this book offered a clear view of the legacies that were being created. Students who attended Hattiesburg schools prior to desegregation shared similar stories and insights regarding their teachers—how they inspired students and taught them well, and were valued mentors and members of the community. Ms. Bettie Dahmer would leave Travillion in 1971, the year of Hattiesburg's desegregation. Once she began attending a desegregated school, her school experiences would shift. The absence of Black educators made her realize the pivotal role that Black women had played in her education and community. Dr. Joyce Ladner credits her teachers with being one of the reasons she came to value learning and reading. Mrs. Jackson was the first example of an intellectual that she had met as a young girl, and this stayed with her. Dr. Anthony Harris echoed this when he spoke about the high expectations his teachers had for him and the motivation they gave him while growing up. Pedagogical practices and relationships were two key components that created positive classroom experiences time and time again.[2] *All* students expressed that their teachers wanted them to learn beyond the books, and that the curriculum was interesting, creative, and connected to real-world learning. From the students' perspective, their learning was meaningful and important.

These students felt that their teachers believed in them, and that this affirmation was vital in shaping their young sense of self. Many of them said they became educators because of the teachers they had. Mrs. Barbara

Elaine Jones shared the story of walking into the classroom on her first day of student teaching and realizing that she would be working with Mrs. Katherine Fowler (one of her former teachers). She was excited and honored to work with Mrs. Fowler, because she wanted to become the type of teacher that Mrs. Fowler was. Thus, the legacy continued.

I Exist Through Legacy

"I exist I exist I exist I exist even though the universe says *no* in iambic pentameter."[3] This existence spans years upon years—it is our legacy.

Black educators were more than educators, as their efforts extended into organizations that supported equal education, civil rights, and activism (e.g., many participants were members of the NAACP or SNCC, and participated in the civil rights movement). In addition to teaching, it would be Black women who helped develop organizations that created comprehensive ways to connect advocacy and education (the Mississippi Association of Educators and a national organization known as the National Association of Teachers in Colored Schools/American Teacher's Association).[4] Jon Hale notes, "The history of teacher organizations in the American South disrupts a narrative of passivity to broaden the conceptualization of civil rights activism to include educators. It also posits that educators organized themselves by following a consistent and coherent agenda of civil rights from the era of Jim Crow through desegregation. Black educators in the South saw their work as political and inherently connected to civil rights. Their subsequent articulation and demand for a right to a quality education contributed significantly to the Civil Rights Movement."[5]

Hale continues, "[T]eachers practiced tenets of intellectual and pedagogical activism that included implementing a curriculum, extracurricular courses, and a culturally relevant education in Black schools during the era of segregation. Teaching behind closed doors and developing their profession inculcated a sense of resistance throughout segregated Black schools across the South that resonated deeply with the principles of the Civil Rights Movement. While not on the front lines of the movement, teachers transformed their profession into a viable and political site of resistance."[6] Teaching behind closed doors allowed educators and principals of Black schools to work collectively despite the local control that white superintendents still exercised over segregated schools. This commitment of time and labor was made evident in the stories heralded by the students who grew up with community support and pedagogical approaches that centered the needs of students. Educators used classrooms and community involvement to create examples for their students to witness. Assuming the role of teacher, activist, organizer, and caretaker embodies what we know today as community and culturally responsive pedagogy. This form of teaching allowed participants to continue the legacy of their teachers, which would be passed on to generations after.

Dr. Joyce Ladner shared that Mrs. Jackson's classroom felt full of possibilities. Mrs. Jackson would tell the class about classical music and expose her students to the joy of reading (e.g., Margaret Walker's poetry). This exposure made Dr. Ladner eager to learn more, and it showed the students the possibilities that existed beyond Mississippi. She recalled a book that described various states and places around the world that Mrs. Jackson had given to her and remembered looking at the pictures and dreaming of one day visiting the places in the book. Such efforts solidified the classroom space as one where real learning could take place. Imagine a barren room, filled with the sounds of students and teacher discussing classical music. I wonder what that classroom must have felt like—Erik Satie's Gymnopédies transporting students to another place, moving between the dissonances and harmonies, or the cadence of Margaret Walker's poem "For My People." There were no bounds to what these women would do to help students learn.

The legacy of these teachers can also be found in the students they inspired and mentored, and the successes that students found after leaving their classrooms. Mrs. Fowler and others mentioned the notable people from Hattiesburg that they recalled:

> Musician Bobby Bryant; Robert Earl James, who has served over fifty years at a Black-owned Bank in Savannah, Georgia; Dr. Walter Massey, President of Morehouse University among his other accolades; Dr. Jimmie James, former Chair of the Music Department at Jackson State University; Jobie Martin, who was the first African American to have his own television show in Mississippi; Dr. Amos Wilson, who was a brilliant author; Mildred Gaddis, radio and television personality; Mayor Johnny Dupree, who served as the first African American mayor of Hattiesburg for sixteen years; and so many others. The University of Southern Mississippi was integrated by two individuals from the segregated Rowan High School, Raylawni Young (Branch), class of 1959 and Elaine Armstrong, class of 1965. Also, William Carey College was desegregated by two Rowan High School graduates from the class of 1965, Lunda Williams and Vermester Jackson (Bester).[7]

Beyond the people mentioned, there are more, because greatness often goes unnoticed and unnamed. This greatness emerged from the legacies created in those small, barren schoolhouses—that were not barren at all thanks to the women who filled them with learning and love. This commitment would ultimately help end Jim Crow and sustain education and activism that changed the landscape of southern life. William Sturkey asserts that "[i]n Hattiesburg and elsewhere, the nature of black activism in the 1960s was inherently different from the activism of previous eras: the civil rights movement of the 1960s directly targeted and successfully overthrew Jim Crow."[8] Black educators and students were part of history through their commitment to education, families, community, and self. Their stories and histories will continue to serve as proof that the Black community, and Black women, will never be silenced. As sociologist Glenn Bracey noted, "Out of the ashes of white denigration, we gave birth to ourselves."[9]

Their commitment and legacies are outlined in the chart below:

Table 3. Additional Data About Participants

Education	Average Years Taught	Students Who Entered the Teaching Field	Activism	Mentorship
95 percent of participants had a master's degree or PhD, despite the barriers to obtaining a college education put up by segregation.	The participants taught an average of thirty-three years.	88 percent of students were inspired by a mentor or educator to enter education or the counseling field.	100 percent of participants consider themselves activists and had some role in the civil rights movement. They credit a mentor/teacher for instilling its importance.	100 percent of participants remained in contact with former students (e.g., Mrs. Jemye Heath would regularly check on Mrs. Armstrong nearly seventy years after having her as a student).

Mrs. Heath, Mrs. Fowler, Mrs. Goins, Mrs. Bobbitt, Mrs. Woullard, Mrs. Hale-Green, Ms. Bettie Dahmer, Mrs. Ellie Dahmer, Dr. Ladner, Mrs. Brown, Mr. Cooper, Mrs. Jones, Mrs. Smith, Mrs. Manning, Mrs. Armstrong, Mrs. Ross, and the many others—your contributions pioneered the way forward. I will add my name to this list of legacy, and other Black and Brown educators will add theirs, as we continue to build on your lives and stories. Our legacies are far too bright to be diminished, and they will continue to shine.

CHAPTER 5

Artifacts and Relics

Our stories and legacies are found in relics. These relics are excavated from the ground, discovered in basements, housed in museums, captured in front-porch conversations. The participants whose stories are included in this book had only a few artifacts in their possession, for example, a yearbook annual from Earl Travillion High School and a copy of the *DePriest Herald*. Historian Kendra Field explains, "There are so many stories about objects that were lost. Lost letters, lost photographs, lost objects of meaning."[10] The images shown in the following pages offer a reclamation and a glimpse into some of the objects that mattered to those attending Black schools and the many Black women who helped lead them, further cementing their legacies and contributions. Mr. Cooper noted that the annuals are important because they capture a time when Black students were editors-in-chief, class presidents, salutatorians—when they could be anything they wanted to be.

The images below are from a yearbook annual created by Black educators and students who used their time, funds (with the help of annual staff and sponsors), and innovation to create something that would not have existed otherwise. Most of the staff who helped put together the annual were women. One image in the annual shows Mrs. Linda Armstrong gathered around a table with eleven other people, working on its pages. Copies of annuals are rare, as many have been lost or destroyed. This annual, though a mere copy made from a mimeograph machine, represents the collective effort of the Black teachers to ensure that their students felt a sense of equality by having a "yearbook" just like the white students did.

Mrs. Armstrong described her very personal vivid memories of the classrooms and schools in a way that further illustrates the importance of the annual:

> I attended DePriest from when I started school until 1957. DePriest was a clapboard school with wooden floors, lumber frame, double door, and big classrooms. The average number of students in a classroom was around twenty-five. The school was in terrible condition, and the students at DePriest did not have a good reputation for attendance. In 1960 I went to high school at Earl Travillion for grades nine through twelve. It was the total opposite of DePriest—a brick building, new, lots of classrooms, and a typing and home economics room. Travillion and DePriest were in Palmers Crossing, which was about five miles from my house—most kids walked or rode their bikes to school. The state knew what it was doing by using the logic of sticking the Black kids in a new school with books that were in a little better shape than those at DePriest. A few

years later, DePriest was shut down. What the state didn't understand was that the building did not really matter. The inside of the building and classroom did not matter. I can still recall the DePriest school song—the dilapidated school that looked as though it should be condemned was still full of what mattered—us.[11]

With the loss and scarcity of artifacts from schools such as DePriest, there is the need to capture the images of the moments and buildings participants referenced.

Mr. Charles Cooper shared that within the community of former Hattiesburg students and teachers today, there are only two known annuals left, one from 1962 and the other from 1956. The images below have been included as a way to make these histories visible and to provide documentation for the lives and experiences of the participants and the sentiments they expressed.

The Travillion school song was written by band director Jimmie James and Helen Dozier, and the school mascot was and still is a tiger. Earl Travillion Attendance Center was built in 1957, after all five Black county schools were combined (DePriest, Bay Springs, Springfield, John White, and Myers), just three years after the *Brown* decision. The five Black county schools were then closed. This meant that all Black students in Forrest County would now attend Earl Travillion. (This would now be the *only* county Black school in Forrest County—this did not include the Black city schools of Forrest County. See the table in chapter 2 for more information.) Although Hattiesburg Public Schools were desegregated in September 1965, Forrest County Schools would not desegregate until 1970. In January of 1971, Black students from Travillion were mandated by the county to attend North Forrest, Petal, or Brooklyn High Schools (white schools), and Travillion became a junior high. According to Charles Cooper, "[d]esegregation in Mississippi meant Black students went to white schools, instead of white students attending Black schools. The class of 1970 of Earl Travillion ordered their caps and gowns because they assumed they would graduate from Earl Travillion, but the county made them attend North Forrest, Petal, or Brooklyn to graduate. They had ordered their caps and gowns and class rings, but it was all for nothing."[12] In Mississippi, currently there are thirty school districts with Department of Justice orders to desegregate (this includes schools in Forrest County), illustrating that these historical inequities remain prevalent today. "According to the DOJ, 30 school districts in Mississippi are currently under such orders. This includes six school districts in the Jackson-metro area and five in the Pine Belt."[13]

Image from Earl Travillion 1962 annual. Courtesy of Mr. Charles Cooper.

Travillion was built to offer the illusion of separate but equal. Resources were better and the facility was new, offering students their first opportunity to have a school library full of books. However, this was at the cost of school closures, and the artifacts within those schools were discarded or lost.

Shown below is a classroom of students and their teacher at Earl Travillion High School in 1962.

Image from Earl Travillion 1962 annual. Library. Special thanks to Dolphin Archival Printing.

Image from Earl Travillion 1962 annual. Classroom.

The Travillion Tiger Booster members were selected by a sponsor (a teacher). The Tiger Boosters performed cheers at various school events. This image is from 1962.

Image from Earl Travillion 1962 annual. Tiger Boosters.

Legacies and Artifacts 123

The images seen in these pages are of Hattiesburg School District teachers and principals from various school years.

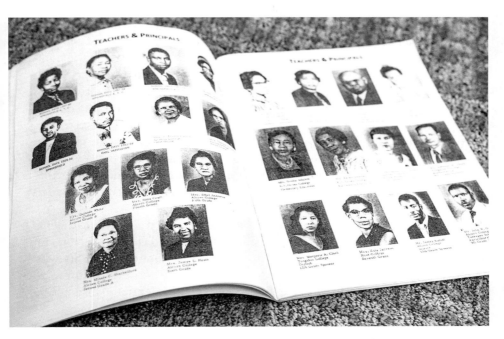

Image from Earl Travillion 1962 annual. Teachers and principals.

Mrs. Zola Jackson, seventh grade teacher, graduate of Rust College.

Image from annual. Mrs. Zola Jackson, seventh grade teacher.

The *DePriest Herald*, 1939

The *DePriest Herald* from 1939 is an artifact that was given to me by Mr. Charles Cooper. His father, Mr. A. C. Cooper, is mentioned in it several times, making it an important piece of history for him. A closer look at the words shows the important role that education played in the community. A section titled "untidiness between the girls and boys" reminds students (and their families) to make sure their appearance is proper and presentable. The care taken when dressing children for school and church was a way to counteract the beliefs of inferiority and second-class citizenship imputed to them, and one that the community took very seriously. In another section of the *DePriest Herald*, "PTA," families are urged to get involved in the schools and community, again illustrating how educators worked in tandem with families to propel efforts for education and civil liberties.

The *DePriest Herald* advertised vocational education classes for students and adults, offered encouragement for community and family involvement, listed absent/truant percentages of schools, and honored students who had academic and sports accolades. Best practices for education were innate, as community involvement was key and differentiated instruction was understood well before its time.

The front page of the *DePriest Herald* reminds its readers that it is a monthly publication and urges them to purchase subscriptions.

The Depriest Herald

DECEMBER 1939

Published Monthly At Forrest County Training School

The Editor's Viewpoint

* * * * *

An Open Letter To Our Reader

Dear Reader!:

As the holiday season approaches, we want to thank you for giving us a grand Christmas.

Your confidence, your ready response and loyal support when we most needed it for our new venture, made THE DEPRIEST HERALD possible. That help was the finest Christmas gift you could have given us.

And now, when you are making up your gift list, if you put your friends down for THE DEPRIEST HERALD as a Christmas gift, you will be sending them something unique, a gift you helped to create, for it was your encouragement and belief that put THE DEPRIEST HERALD on top.

This magazine of yours is one of the outstanding gifts of the year:

A gift that has become most popular—
A gift that is timely, resourceful, educational—
A gift that will renew itself month after month throughout the year as a reminder of your Christmas thought—

Since you had so much to do with the success of THE DEPRIEST HERALD through your own subscription, I think you will find it hard to imagine a more personal, a more useful, or a more timely gift for anyone. And harder still to find a gift more economical, for THE DEPRIEST HERALD subscribers can enter gift subscriptions for their friends this Christmas at the rate of 65c a year and 50c for the remainder of school year.

THE DEPRIEST HERALD is such an easy gift to give, far from the struggle and strain of Christmas shopping crowds. Just write your gift list, slip it into an envelope, and mail it today.

THE DEPRIEST HERALD does the rest. When Christmas comes the first gift copy will be delivered, and your gift will be announced by a beautiful Christmas card. Your name will be written on the card with the words that you are sending THE DEPRIEST HERALD for Christmas.

I hope the friends on your Christmas gift list will enjoy THE DEPRIEST HERALD each month next year as much as you are enjoying it.

ELMO G. CONEY, Director

Image from *DePriest Herald*, 1939. Courtesy of Mr. Charles Cooper.

An illustration of the time taken to care for the whole child, and the collective approach of doing so, from 1939.

> ### "UNTIDINESS AMONG THE GIRLS AND BOYS"
>
> Girls and boys should come to school neatly dressed, not saying to wear your best clothes, but you can take what you have and make it look nice and neat. As girls you should darn your hose or do whatever has to be done to your clothes the night before.
>
> Girls who have small sisters should help their mothers to look after them. See that they are neatly dressed, in every respect before they leave home. Girls should see that their hair is properly cared for before going to the classroom. Do not wait until you are in the classroom to see that your hair hasn't had the proper care or your face hasn't had a powder puff on it for at least a half day.
>
> Young men, you should not wear your best clothes to school, but you should try to look your best before going out. You are to be the men to tomorrow, because once you acquire the habit of dressing neatly you will always want to look that way. Don't come to school looking like a man going to work, because here you meet your neighbors of tomorrow. It is quite alright to play basketball but please do not wear your sweat shirt under your dress shirt because your friends cannot stay around you. If you have a coat wear it to school, and if it is torn, don't pin it up with a pin but don the garment, before coming to school—or one should not wear the garment at all.
>
> If you have a sister, ask her to darn the garment, if not, darn the garment yourself, because your sister will not be with you always.
>
> Girls shouldn't wear a torn dress to school, neither torn hose. Because "a stitch in time saves nine." Before going out ask yourself these questions:
> "Is my face clean?"
> "Is my neck clean?"
> "Are my ears clean?"
> "Are my teeth clean?"
> "Have I a clean handkerchief?"
> "Is my hair bushed?"
> "Am I ready for school?"
> "Have I given myself the proper care, in order to look neatly among others?"
>
> Note to Parents: Watch your child's appearance when they leave to go to school in the mornngi
>
> L. Robinson, DeElla Csism.

Image from *DePriest Herald*, 1939.

DePriest was one of the five county schools that closed in 1957 when Travillion opened. All that is left of DePriest is the cafeteria, which still stands today. Many participants who attended DePriest had fond memories of it. The image below displays the buildings of DePriest.

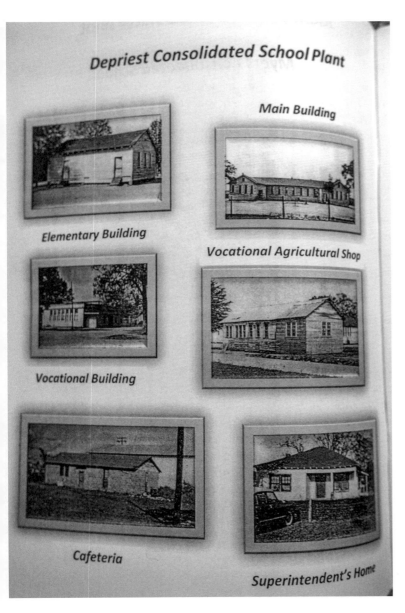

Image from FORDETRA book. DePriest school buildings. Courtesy of Mr. Charles Cooper.

HISTORICAL VIGNETTE
Christopher M. Span

Long-Standing Legacies

Reflecting on the educators discussed in this book and their relentless dedication to advancing knowledge while uplifting youth and communities to their fullest potential, one cannot overlook the deeply ingrained roots of such efforts in Mississippi, spanning back over a century. Even before Emancipation, which arrived a few years earlier in Mississippi compared to other southern states, the seeds of resistance against slavery were sown through the establishment of schools and the search for educators who could impart knowledge and sow the seeds of freedom in young minds.

The most powerful tool of liberation during Emancipation was literacy—a foundation upon which freedom, knowledge, and social mobility could be built. It was quietly cultivated within the slave community, but its true essence blossomed with Emancipation. This legacy reflects the relentless pursuit of progress spanning at least five generations of African Americans in Mississippi. They steadfastly believed in the potential for societal advancement through education and recognized the pivotal role of teachers in realizing this vision.

Yet, alongside this movement for freedom, there existed a stark reality—the pervasive limitations imposed by a society steeped in racial discrimination. Some chose to leave, contributing to the outmigration known as the Great Migration, seeking opportunities elsewhere while still holding on to their roots in Mississippi. However, for those who remained, their decision symbolized a commitment to confronting the challenges head-on and educating others on navigating the treacherous landscape of Jim Crow Mississippi.

In this narrative, the significance of women emerges prominently. As the teaching profession became increasingly gendered, Black women assumed pivotal roles both within their families and communities and as educators. Their empowerment to advocate for the betterment of their communities was not an anomaly but a consistent thread woven throughout history, often overlooked but integral to the fabric of societal progress.

As we contemplate these untold stories and overlooked heroes, it becomes evident that the role of teachers transcends mere instruction—they are catalysts for change, central to the collective pursuit of a more just and equitable society. In recognizing their contributions within the broader context of Mississippi's history, we acknowledge both the debts owed to past generations and the aspirations for a brighter future, where opportunity and equality prevail. The intersection of the research in this book with the backdrop of desegregation in Mississippi underscores the essential nature of this narrative in shaping our collective understanding of history.

Aliyah Bonnette, *They Just Want a Sip from Your Water*, 2022. Quilt with oil, beading, and applique. "I taught myself quilting to physically connect to my grandmother and the practices of my women ancestors. By incorporating the very fabrics and unfinished quilts she touched and sewed, my practice becomes a space to stitch together the stories and memories of black women across generations. My work tells the story of a black woman's journey to find herself. The figures within my work are women living in comfortable environments where they may reveal their authentic self."

POETIC REFLECTION

A Place for Fire[14]

Jordan Stempleman

I first found the words by pointing

at those old sayings the midsized shadows

that bind the faults clean

this is now the time when the inaction

moves beyond this silence this what survives

so free to seek sound

You said learning isn't so much

prevention but the process to no longer

almost begin again

and our waiting when unwaited is what acts

what acts against that broken-down defense

to have it all

EPILOGUE

Listening to the Lessons

The struggle is eternal. The tribe increases.
Somebody else carries on.
—Ella Baker

Kevin Hopkins, *Congratulations Dr. Ladner*, 2022. Fabric and paint. This artwork was based on an image of Joyce Ladner from her high school graduation in Hattiesburg, Mississippi.

Lessons

Black female teachers in Hattiesburg were successful in educating students despite unfavorable social and school conditions, lack of resources, and the racial climate in the Jim Crow South. In addition to the high expectations they had, these teachers educated the whole child and were integral in ensuring that the Black community thrived. They were creative, loving, and strict, and they worked tirelessly to educate both themselves and their students. They were freedom fighters for education, for the Black community, for voting rights, and for racial equality. They embodied resistance and regality through their selfless acts to eradicate inequality and lift students up.

Oral histories and accounts such as those shared by participants remind us that we need to listen to their lessons. Desegregation was finally implemented in 1970, and over the years from 1964 to 1972 "close to a third of the nation's Black teaching force lost their jobs."[1] This loss of talented veteran teaching staff and the sense of community they encouraged is still felt in America today. We see the ripple effect of this history, as school districts struggle to maintain a diverse teaching staff that mirrors the growing diversity of the student population. As Vanessa Siddle Walker says, "By and large, this culture of black teaching died with *Brown*."[2]

As a nation, we must examine why we have not considered the lessons that can be gained from the contributions of Black female educators. Moving forward, how do we remind ourselves to align the future and the society we want to see with the amplification of the voices most worthy and notable? Oral histories are vast, and Black women are the voices of deep generational knowledge. If we want an inclusive America, these voices must be at the forefront of our country's historical narrative.

Where Do We Go from Here?

The loss of Black school buildings, artifacts, stories, and histories illustrates the dismantling of Black spaces and Black memories. The Black women who led these classrooms are in many ways at risk of vanishing from the stories collected around our history. Who should have autonomy in schools, and how does this "history of time forgotten" currently impact our classrooms and curricula and academia itself? Today, we are seeing the lasting impact of our pasts.

Professor Erica Frankenberg states:

> Today, according to a 2022 federal report, 46% of public school students are white, 28% are Hispanic, 15% are Black, 6% Asian, 4% multiracial and 1% American Indian. And yet, public schools are deeply segregated. In 2021, approximately 60% of Black and Hispanic public school students attended schools where 75% or more of students were students of color. A 2019 report by EdBuild, a nonprofit that produced reports on school funding inequities, found that schools in predominantly nonwhite districts received $23 billion less in funding each year than schools in majority white districts. This equates to roughly $2,200 less per student per year. Unequal funding results in less student access to advanced, college-prep courses, to name just one example.[3]

Reform is necessary if we hope to ensure equitable education for students and build on past efforts. "Unlearning the hush" asks us to examine the past and ourselves to best inform our future practices in education.[4] Using oral histories and the experiences of participants as the foundation of our action is a critical piece of this work. We must determine how we can work toward including such histories in our classrooms, as well as mandating inclusive and equitable curriculum, working collectively to advocate for reform, and illuminating marginalized or silenced histories. Guided by these histories, we can have a more accurate understanding of ourselves and others; understanding them helps us further the work and vision of the everyday heroes that came before us. In the words of SNCC member Martha Prescod Norman Noonan: "When all is said and done, it shouldn't be left to history to give our children a sense of us, because we're still here."[5] We are most certainly still here, and we need to address the racial disparities and inequities that continue to exist in our school system and classrooms.

We are being carried on the backs of these legacies and these women, our ancestry. Let us remember their collective efforts and contributions and continue to tell their stories and histories for generations to come, to build bridges and rehumanize our connections to self and others.

POETIC REFLECTION

Some Years There Exists a Wanting to Escape
Claudia Rankine[6]

Some years there exists a wanting to escape—

you, floating above your certain ache—

still the ache coexists.

Call that the immanent you—

You are you even before you

grow into understanding you

are not anyone, worthless,

not worth you.

Even as your own weight insists
you are here, fighting off
the weight of nonexistence.

And still this life parts your lids, you see
you seeing your extending hand

as a falling wave—

/

I they he she we you turn
only to discover
the encounter

to be alien to this place.

Wait.

The patience is in the living. Time opens out to you.

The opening, between you and you, occupied,
zoned for an encounter,

given the histories of you and you—

And always, who is this you?

The start of you, each day,
a presence already—

Hey you—

/

Slipping down burying the you buried within. You are everywhere and you are nowhere in the day.

The outside comes in—

Then you, hey you—

Overheard in the moonlight.

Overcome in the moonlight.

Soon you are sitting around, publicly listening, when you hear this—what happens to you doesn't belong to you, only half concerns you He is speaking of the legionnaires in Claire Denis's film *Beau Travail* and you are pulled back into the body of you receiving the nothing gaze—

The world out there insisting on this only half concerns you. What happens to you doesn't belong to you, only half concerns you. It's not yours. Not yours only.

/

And still a world begins its furious erasure—

Who do you think you are, saying I to me?

You nothing.

You nobody.

You.

A body in the world drowns in it—

Hey you—

All our fevered history won't instill insight,
won't turn a body conscious,
won't make that look
in the eyes say yes, though there is nothing

to solve

even as each moment is an answer.

/

Don't say I if it means so little,
holds the little forming no one.

You are not sick, you are injured—

you ache for the rest of life.

How to care for the injured body,

the kind of body that can't hold
the content it is living?

And where is the safest place when that place
must be someplace other than in the body?

Even now your voice entangles this mouth
whose words are here as pulse, strumming
shut out, shut in, shut up—

You cannot say—

A body translates its you—

you there, hey you

/

even as it loses the location of its mouth.

When you lay your body in the body
entered as if skin and bone were public places,

when you lay your body in the body
entered as if you're the ground you walk on,

you know no memory should live
in these memories

becoming the body of you.

You slow all existence down with your call
detectable only as sky. The night's yawn
absorbs you as you lie down at the wrong angle

to the sun ready already to let go of your hand.

Wait with me
though the waiting, wait up,
might take until nothing whatsoever was done.

/

To be left, not alone, the only wish—

to call you out, to call out you.

Who shouted, you? You

shouted you, you the murmur in the air, you sometimes sounding like you, you sometimes saying you,

go nowhere,

be no one but you first—

Nobody notices, only you've known,

you're not sick, not crazy,
not angry, not sad—

It's just this, you're injured.

/

Everything shaded everything darkened everything Shadowed

is the stripped is the struck—

is the trace
is the aftertaste.

I they he she we you were too concluded yesterday to know whatever was done could also be done, was also done, was never done—

The worst injury is feeling you don't belong so much

to you—

Audio Poems

Never forget where we came from and always praise the bridges that carried us over.
—Fannie Lou Hamer

"Hear it. Here we are standing."[1]

• • •

Poems are meant to be heard, and I invite you to listen to the poems found in this book. A link to the audio files of the poems can be found at the University of Illinois Press website and accessed through the supplemental material tab on the web page for the book. The poems are narrated by Ashley M. Jones, poet laureate of Alabama, leaving us with lasting words and images of hope.

Mario Joyce, *A Light Change (June Bug)*, 2023. Photographed by Mario Joyce and Sakhile&Me. "The soil from the farm I grew up on (though visible) holds an unseen pull, and evidence of historical pulls, some measurable and others eluding capture. I am studying the properties within these soil time capsules in the form of stories, while investigating the DNA of the soil I grew up on and how it fused with my young, fragile genome."

POETIC REFLECTION

What If I Told You, He Grew Up[1]
Michelle Taransky

In a house without books where he was never
Read to. But he taught me

To protect me and all I know
About how to be safe
Is writing a book.

When my kids come home
From school they can't tell
The teachers from me
I want them to say mother

I am glad when my husband calls me
Annie Hall. It's the same day I like how my mom's friends
Like every single picture I post
Individually

You know, someone has to check-in
On all the chickens

I want to find something other
Amid the kvetching, aggression, resistance
And subversion I am not distracted, I am lost

In content and happy you are self
Diagnosing

How do I keep my children's memories

Stocked with memory aids

I made them

Include signposts, saying

Again and again: we aren't accustomed to

Reading this way

Some genre will be our duck and cover

If we want security theater

I didn't write a book

I called *Beloved*

But I saw them all over the internet

I didn't expect the student

Poem about lighting the

Candles to be so difficult to comment on

I can't still am not getting past

That first sentence

There's some research in poetry studies

About the recent thoughts we're having

Busy work versus

I dreamt of the definite

Conclusion like this

Last year

Abbreviations and People List

Abbreviations

BIPOC	Black/Indigenous/Persons of Color
CEP	Citizenship Education Program
COFO	Council of Federated Organizations
CORE	Congress of Racial Equity
FORDETRA	Forrest County/DePriest/Travillion Hattiesburg Schools Reunion Group, which was formed in the 1990s. There are approximately one hundred members, who participate in reunions and in preserving past artifacts and Hattiesburg history.
HBCU	Historically Black College or University
MATCS	Mississippi Association of Teachers in Colored Schools
MCEE	Mississippi Citizens Council on Education
MEA	Mississippi Education Association
NAACP	National Association for the Advancement of Colored People
NATCS	National Association of Teachers in Colored Schools
NCNW	National Council of Negro Women
NEA	National Education Association
SCLC	Southern Christian Leadership Conference
SNCC	Student Nonviolent Coordinating Committee

People (not an exhaustive list)

Armstrong, Linda—Participant, student at Forrest County Schools, daughter of educator Zola Jackson, and mother of author.

Bobbitt, Mary—Participant, mentor, and special education educator.

Brown, Julia—Participant, student at Forrest County Schools, counselor, and activist from Hattiesburg.

Bunch, Lonnie—The 14th Secretary of the Smithsonian, educator, author, and cousin of the author's husband (Damian Bunch).

Cooper, Charles—Participant, student at Forrest County Schools, and educator.

Dahmer, Bettie—Participant, activist, student at Forrest County Schools, and daughter of Ellie and Vernon Dahmer.

Dahmer, Ellie Jewell—Participant, educator, and activist who helped advocate for voter registration. Mrs. Dahmer taught for many years in segregated Forrest County schools.

Dahmer, Vernon F.—Civil rights activist from Hattiesburg who worked to ensure voting rights.

Evers, Medgar—The NAACP's first field secretary. He worked to help integrate the University of Mississippi and bring equality to Mississippi schools and laws.

Fowler, Katherine—Participant, educator, mentor, and activist in Hattiesburg.

Goins, Eleanor Deloris—Participant, educator and principal, FORDETRA member, and activist.

Hale-Green, Carolyn—Participant, student at Hattiesburg Public Schools and counselor in Hattiesburg Public Schools.

Harris, Anthony—Participant, student at Hattiesburg Public Schools, educator, activist, student at Freedom Schools, and author.

Heath, Jemye—Participant, educator, principal, mentor, and activist from Hattiesburg. Rest in power, Mrs. Heath.

Jackson, Zola—Educator, mother of participant Linda Armstrong, and grandmother of the author.

Jones, Barbara Elaine—Participant, educator, and activist of Hattiesburg.

Kennard, Clyde—Civil rights leader and war veteran from Hattiesburg. He was framed for a false charge and spent time in Parchment Penitentiary, where he died of cancer.

Ladner, Dorie—Civil rights activist, SNCC member, founding member of the Council of Federated Organizations (COFO), and sister of Joyce Ladner.

Ladner, Joyce—Participant, civil rights activist, sociologist, educator, SNCC member, author of *Tomorrow's Tomorrow* (among other books), and sister of Dorie Ladner.

Massey, Walter—Educator and physicist. He served as the director for the National Science Foundation and former vice president of the American Physical Society. He attended Hattiesburg schools.

Smith, Jeanette—Civil rights activist. She served on the county NAACP and was also elected to the county election commission.

Span, Christopher—Historian of education, educator, author, and mentor. He is also the Dean and Distinguished Professor of the Graduate School of Education at Rutgers.

Woullard, Juruthin (Rosetta)—Participant, educator and principal.

Notes

Poetic Reflections and Preface and Origin Story

1. Ariana Benson, "Elders Speak of the Windchimes." The poem first appeared in her book *The Black Pastoral*, featured in *The Georgia Review* (Winter 2023). Benson was awarded the Lenore Marshall Poetry Prize for best poetry book of the year.

2. Siddle Walker, "School 'Outer-Gration' and 'Tokenism,'" 111–24.

3. Recent authors have offered important historical information about the role of Black educators. This research builds upon past scholarship offering a specific focus on Mississippi educators.

4. Throughout this book I have intentionally used language that elevates Black women and works against tropes and misnomers. Words such as phenomenal, trailblazers, etc., have not been historically associated with Black women. It is time to activate language that associates Black women with greatness, expertise, and owners of knowledge.

5. Milner, "The Promise of Black Teachers' Success with Black Students," 89–104.

6. Glassie, "The Practice and Purpose of History," 966.

7. Payne, *I've Got the Light of Freedom*, 392.

8. Payne, *I've Got the Light of Freedom*, 393.

9. Ladner, *Tomorrow's Tomorrow*, xxiii.

10. Berrey, "Resistance Begins at Home," 65–90.

11. Kelley, "'We Are Not What We Seem,'" 79.

12. Gavins, "Literature on Jim Crow," 13, 14.

13. Mr. Charles Cooper, interview by author, October 2024.

14. Mary Ruefle, "A Certain Swirl," from her collection *The Most of It* (Wave Books 2008).

Chapter 1. "Everybody Knows about Mississippi"

1. Evie Shockley, "statistical hailu (or, how do they discount us? let me count the ways)," from *the new black* (Wesleyan University Press, 2012).
2. Fairclough, "'Being in the Field of Education and Also Being a Negro... Seems... Tragic,'" 77–97.
3. Givens, "What's Missing from the Discourse about Anti-Racist Teaching."
4. Siddle Walker, "Black Educators as Educational Advocates in the Decades before *Brown v. Board of Education*," 217.
5. Funchess, "Hattiesburg Schools Desegregation Took 10 Years."
6. Fields, "The Story behind Nina Simone's Protest Song, 'Mississippi Goddam.'"
7. Shankar, "'People Who Stood Up.'"
8. Siddle Walker, "African American Teaching in the South," 751–79.
9. Burrow, "Mississippi Made to Disappear," in *A Child Shall Lead Them*, 144–216.
10. NAACP, "History of Lynching in America," February 11, 2022, https://naacp.org/find-resources/history-explained/history-lynching-america, 2.
11. Houck, "Killing Emmett," 1.
12. Jon Hale, "A History of the Mississippi Freedom Schools, 1954–1965" (dissertation, ProQuest, 2009), 17.
13. Hale, *A History of the Mississippi Freedom Schools, 1954–1965*, 43; Hale, "'The Development of Power Is the Main Business of the School,'" 444–59.
14. Carney, "The Vestiges of Jim Crow and the Mississippi Sovereignty Commission."
15. Funchess, "Hattiesburg Schools Desegregation Took 10 Years."
16. Bolton, "*Mississippi's School Equaiiztion Program, 1945–1954*," 1.
17. Mississippi Statistical Abstract, 171.
18. U.S. Census Bureau, "Mississippi 2020 Census," Census.gov, October 8, 2021, https://www.census.gov/library/stories/state-by-state/mississippi-population-change-between-census-decade.html.
19. Sturkey, *Hattiesburg*, 50.
20. Charles Payne, "Testing the Limits," in *I've Got the Light of Freedom*, 29–66.
21. Mosnier, "Dorie Ann Ladner and Joyce Ladner Oral History Interview Conducted by Joseph Mosnier in Washington, DC, September 20, 2011." See the index of abbreviations and persons for additional information about Dorie Ladner, Vernon Dahmer, and others.
22. Fordetra Reunion Book.
23. There is recognition that not all Black educators in Mississippi were excellent. However, this book's participants estimated that 85 to 90 percent of the Black educators they encountered were excellent and left a lasting impact.
24. Sturkey, *Hattiesburg*, 173.

25. Ariana Benson, "Love Poem in the Black Field." The poem first appeared in her book *The Black Pastoral*, featured in *The Georgia Review* (Winter 2023).

Chapter 2. The Wisdom of Elders

1. Emily Pettit, "Cartography," 2023. Poem first published in *Unlearning the Hush*.
2. Payne, *I've Got the Light of Freedom*, 29.
3. Alex Haley, Black History, Oral History and Genealogy, September 4, 2018. https://alexhaley.com/2018/08/06/black-history-oral-history-and-genealogy/.
4. Secretary Lonnie Bunch, interview by author, October 2021. The full quote is found in his oral history.
5. In Perks and Thomson, *The Oral History Reader*, 52.
6. In Perks and Thomson, *The Oral History Reader*, 34.
7. Stewart, "Lonnie G. Bunch III."
8. Trescott, Lonnie Bunch interview, *Washington Post*.
9. Secretary Lonnie Bunch, interview by author, May 2021.
10. Secretary Lonnie Bunch, interview by author, May 2021.
11. Ms. Bettie Dahmer, interview by author, January 12, 2024.
12. Dr. Anthony Harris, interview by author, October 22, 2023.
13. Mrs. Julia Brown, interview by author, December 26, 2023.
14. Mr. Charles Cooper, interview by author, February 2022.
15. Mrs. Barbara Elaine Jones, interview by author, January 7, 2024.
16. The White Citizens' Council was a group of white men who worked against integration and were known to have racist ideologies and policies that diminished the hopes of Black educators for a fair desegregation.
17. The Spirit was a group of Black community members that made sure that the community supported efforts for activism and equality. Mrs. Goins shared that if, for example, the community was boycotting a white-owned store that would not hire Black employees, and a Black community member shopped there, the Spirit would pay them a visit.
18. Mrs. Eleanor Deloris Goins, interview by author, August 2021.
19. Mrs. Mary Lewis Bobbitt, interview by author, July 2021.
20. Mrs. Linda Armstrong, interview by author, June 2021.
21. Dr. Joyce Ladner, interview by author, May 2021.
22. Mrs. Carolyn Hale-Green, interview by author, August 2021.
23. Mrs. Juruthin (Rosetta) Woullard, interview by author, May 2021.
24. Mrs. Katherine Fowler, interview by author, August 2021.
25. Mrs. Jemye Heath, interview by author, March 2021. Rest in love and power, Mrs. Heath.
26. Mrs. Linda Armstrong, speaking about Zola Jackson, interview by author, October 2024.

27. Mrs. Ellie Jewell Davis Dahmer, interview by author, January 11, 2024.

28. Nate Marshall, "On Caskets," which appeared previously in *Poetry Magazine*, April 2015.

Chapter 3. Unwavering Determination

1. Jordan Stempleman, "Lessons," 2024. A version of "Lessons" first appeared in the *Laurel Review*, 2023.

2. William Sturkey discusses the function of schools in segregated communities and how they served as bridges for events, meetings, fundraisers, ceremonies, lectures, and so forth.

3. Berrey, "Resistance Begins at Home," 67. The research of Stephen Berrey, Patricia Hill Collins, and Tamara Beauboeuf-Lafontant offers context for how women navigated their agency.

4. Beauboeuf-Lafontant, "A Womanist Experience of Caring," 71–86.

5. Berrey, "Resistance Begins at Home," 67–68.

6. Berrey, "Resistance Begins at Home," 70.

7. The concept of duality can be further explored in *Souls of Black Folk* by W. E. B. Du Bois.

8. Collins, "The Politics of Black Feminist Thought," in *Black Feminist Thought*, 3–27.

9. Berrey, "Resistance Begins at Home," 79.

10. Sturkey, *Hattiesburg*, 296–98.

11. Segregation Is Constitutional but Compulsory Integration Is Unconstitutional, n.d., box 1135. Social Documents Collection, msc1075. University of Iowa Special Collections. https://aspace.lib.uiowa.edu/repositories/2/archival_objects/840750.

12. The literature on the massive resistance movement and its many local and state varieties is vast. See, for example, Numan Bartley, *The Rise of Massive Resistance: Race and Politics in the South during the 1950s* (Baton Rouge: Louisiana State University Press, 1969), 77; Benjamin Muse, *Ten Years of Prelude: The Story of Integration Since the Supreme Court's 1954 Decision* (New York: Viking Press, 1964), 39; Reed Sarratt, *The Ordeal of Desegregation: The First Decade* (New York: Harper and Row, 1966); *The Moderates' Dilemma: Massive Resistance to School Desegregation in Virginia*, eds. Matthew Lassiter and Andrew B. Lewis (Charlottesville: University Press of Virginia, 1998). The four states that abolished their state constitutional requirements for public education were Georgia, Alabama, Mississippi, and South Carolina; the six states that passed legislation denying funds to desegregated schools were Arkansas, Georgia, Louisiana, Mississippi, South Carolina, and Virginia. See Davison Douglas, "The Rhetoric of Moderation: Desegregating the South During the Decade After *Brown*," *Northwestern University Law Review* 89, no. 92 (1994): 92–137.

13. Fultz, "The Displacement of Black Educators Post-*Brown*," 15. The *Brown II* decision in 1955 was meant to ensure that separate schools for Blacks and whites were dismantled. This decision was met with various forms of resistance.

14. Sturkey, *Hattiesburg*, 251–69.

15. Fultz, "The Displacement of Black Educators Post-*Brown*," 13–14.

16. Fultz, "The Displacement of Black Educators Post-*Brown*," 14.

17. Fairclough, "'Being in the Field of Education and Also Being a Negro . . . Seems . . . Tragic,'" 65–91.

18. As Christopher M. Span notes, "For more than a century, scholars—more specifically, African American scholars—have written on the expansion of slavery, its impact on the making of the African American family and culture, and the role kinfolk (family) played in African Americans surviving nearly 250 years of enslavement. W. E. B. Du Bois was among the first to combine history, autoethnography, and storytelling to explain the multiple layers of consciousness of the Black past, and how these layers of consciousness became strategies of survival in the present. Others would follow, such as John Hope Franklin, James Baldwin, Sterling Stuckey, Alex Haley, Maya Angelou, Toni Morrison, Virginia Hamilton, Jason R. Young, and Ta-Nehisi Coates. In the African American tradition, as Virginia Hamilton reminds us in her children's books [*The Planet of Junior Brown* and *M. C. Higgins, the Great*, among others], 'storytelling was the first opportunity for black folk to represent themselves as anything other than property.' To story-tell is to bear witness. For African Americans—then and now—it is their way of saying I am here, was here, and I matter(ed)." "Sam's Cottonfield Blues," 10.

19. Fultz, "African American Teachers in the South," 401–22.

20. Siddle Walker, "Askwith Forums Black Educators and the Struggle for Justice in Schools." Siddle Walker overviews the manner in which educators used organization and collective efforts to make the curriculum a space for equitable learning.

21. Collins, *Black Feminist Thought*, 101–2. Collins's use of safe spaces does not discount the threat of violence in Jim Crow South but recognizes the influence and power of the family unit, the community, and the spaces that sought to counter the messages of racist laws and ideologies.

22. Ladner, *The Ties That Bind*, 120–22.

23. Gaines and Abrams, *The Class of 1968*, 81.

24. Funchess, "Hattiesburg Schools Desegregation Took 10 Years." Additional information was gained from my multiple interviews with Mr. Charles Cooper.

25. Maxine Chernoff, "Miss Banks," 2024. Written for *Unlearning the Hush*.

Chapter 4. Love Is Resistance

1. Cole Swensen, "Haint Blue." This poem first appeared in *Gravesend* and has been printed here with the author's and publisher's permission. Swensen is a poet, editor, and translator. She has received multiple awards for her work.
2. Ladner, *The Ties That Bind*, 38.
3. Siddle Walker, "Valued Segregated Schools," 265.
4. Siddle Walker, "Valued Segregated Schools," 265.
5. Eleanor Deloris Goins, interview by author, April 2022. Mrs. Goins could not attend University of Southern Mississippi or William Carey College because Blacks were not allowed, so she went to Alcorn State University for her bachelor's degree and then attended William Carey after it became integrated for her master's degree in education.
6. Siddle Walker, "Valued Segregated Schools," 266.
7. Sturkey, *Hattiesburg*, 296.
8. Terry Kawi, "The Importance of Windows and Mirrors in Stories," PBS, June 20, 2022. https://www.pbs.org/education/blog/the-importance-of-windows-and-mirrors-in-stories. Windows and mirrors is a term coined by Rudine Sims Bishop. The term refers to the ways that people see themselves and others. A mirror allows you to see yourself reflected, and a window gives you ways to view the world. The term is often used when considering representation in literature, classrooms, and so forth.
9. Givens, "What's Missing from the Discourse about Anti-Racist Teaching."
10. Alridge, Hale, and Loder-Jackson, *Schooling the Movement*, 16.
11. Hale, "'We Are Not Merging on an Equal Basis,'" 463–81.
12. Breathett, "Black Educators and the United States Supreme Court Decision *Brown versus the Board of Education*," 201–8.
13. Madkins, "The Black Teacher Shortage," 417–27.
14. Ethridge, "Impact of the 1954 Brown vs. Topeka Board of Education Decision on Black Educators," 219–22.
15. Juruthin Rosetta Woullard, interview by author, May 2021.
16. Siddle Walker, "Valued Segregated Schools," 253–85.
17. Morris and Morris, *The Price They Paid*.
18. Siddle Walker, "Black Educators as Educational Advocates," 207–22.
19. Tillman, "(Un)Intended Consequences of *Brown*," 280–303.
20. Eleanor Deloris Goins, interview by author, August 2021.
21. Mary Bobbitt, interview by author, April 2021.
22. Lonnie Bunch, interview by author, October 14, 2021.
23. Span, *From Cotton Field to Schoolhouse*, 46.
24. Marcucci, "Zora Neale Hurston and the *Brown* Debate," 13–24.
25. Milner and Howard, "Black Teachers, Black Students, Black Communities, and *Brown*," 285–95.
26. Mary Bobbitt, interview by author, April 2021.
27. Charles Cooper, interview by author, October 2024.

28. Linda Armstrong, interview by author, June 2021.
29. Mary Bobbitt, interview by author, April 2021.
30. Linda Armstrong, interview by author, June 2021.
31. Berrey, "Resistance Begins at Home," 65–90.
32. Siddle Walker, "Black Educators as Educational Advocates."
33. Linda Armstrong, interview by author, June 2021.
34. Siddle Walker, *Their Highest Potential*, 265–66.
35. Hale, "'The Development of Power Is the Main Business of the School,'" 445.
36. Linda Armstrong, interview by author, June 2021.
37. Linda Armstrong, interview by author, June 2021.
38. Eleanor Deloris Goins, interview by author, August 2021.
39. Siddle Walker, "Valued Segregated Schools," 125.
40. Katherine Fowler, interview by author, August 2021.
41. Carolyn Hale-Green, interview by author, August 2021.
42. Alva Manning, interview by author, August 2021.
43. Carolyn Hale-Green, interview by author, August 2021.
44. Heller, "Telling the Untold Stories of School Integration: An Interview with Vanessa Siddle Walker," 44.
45. Eleanor Deloris Goins, interview by author, August 2021.
46. Heller, "Telling the Untold Stories of School Integration: An Interview with Vanessa Siddle Walker," 4.
47. Ladner, *The Ties That Bind*, 25.
48. Stanley Banks, Annihilation No. 7–11. Originally published in *Blue Beat Syncopation* (2002) and *Memories & Memoirs* (2000) 8.

Chapter 5. Legacies and Artifacts

1. Ashley M. Jones, "African American Literature I," 2022. Published for the first time in *Unlearning the Hush*. Ashley M. Jones is the poet laureate of Alabama (2022–26). She narrates poems you can listen to using the QR code in the Audio Poems section of the book.
2. The universality of these practices and relationships is not being discussed, but rather a focus on educators in this book and in Hattiesburg.
3. Line from Jones's poem "African American Literature I."
4. Perry, *History of the American Teachers Association*.
5. Hale, "'The Development of Power Is the Main Business of the School,'" 446.
6. Hale, "'The Development of Power Is the Main Business of the School,'" 454.
7. Katherine Fowler, interview by author, August 2021.
8. Sturkey, *Hattiesburg*, 296.
9. Jones, "Our Democracy's Founding Ideals Were False When They Were Written," 359–82. Jones quotes Glenn Bracey on page 17 of the article.

10. Kendra Field, "Things to Be Forgotten: Time, Place, and Silence in African American Family Histories," from her lecture at the Berkshire Conference of Women Historians, 2019.

11. Linda Armstrong, interview by author, August 2021.

12. Charles Cooper, interview by author, December 2024.

13. Grove, "Mississippi Has 30 School Districts with Desegregation Orders."

14. Jordan Stempleman, "A Place for Fire," 2023. First published in *Unlearning the Hush*.

Epilogue

1. Rizga, "What If Teachers Didn't Focus So Much on Individual Achievement?"

2. Vanessa Siddle Walker, quoted in Toppo, "Thousands of Black Teachers Lost Jobs."

3. Frankenberg, "70 Years After Brown vs. Board of Education, Public Schools Still Deeply Segregated."

4. Irvine, "An Analysis of the Problem of Disappearing Black Educators," 503–13.

5. Martha P. Noonan, interviewed by John Dittmer; Nasstrom, "Between Memory and History," 325.

6. Claudia Rankine, "Some Years There Exists a Wanting to Escape," in *Citizen: An American Lyric*. Graywolf Press, 2014. Reprinted with the permission of The Permissions Company, LLC on behalf of Graywolf Press, Minneapolis, Minnesota, graywolfpress.org.

Audio Poems

1. Line from Emily Pettit's poem "Cartography," 2024. The poem first appeared in *Unlearning the Hush*.

Poetic Reflection by Michelle Taransky

1. Michelle Taransky, "What If I Told You, He Grew Up," 2024. First published in *Unlearning the Hush*.

Bibliography

Primary Sources

ARCHIVES

Jackson, Mississippi
Hattiesburg American Newspaper Archives
Hattiesburg, Mississippi Earl Travillion Annual
Mississippi Department of Archives and History (MDAH)
National Archives
National Education Association
Oral History Association
University of Southern Mississippi McCain Library and Archives
U.S. Census Bureau

ORAL HISTORY INTERVIEWS

Mrs. Linda Armstrong
Secretary Lonnie Bunch
Mrs. Mary Lewis Bobbitt
Ms. Julia Brown
Mr. Charles Cooper
Mrs. Ellie Davis Dahmer
Ms. Bettie Dahmer
Dr. Anthony Harris
Mrs. Jemye Heath
Mrs. Elaine Jones
Dr. Joyce Ladner
Mrs. Katherine Fowler
Mrs. Eleanor Deloris Goins
Mrs. Carolyn Hale-Green

Mrs. Alva Manning
Mrs. Barbara Ross
Mrs. Freddye Smith
Mrs. Juruthin (Rosetta) Woullard

ADDITIONAL INTERVIEWS AND CONVERSATIONS

Dr. Derrick Alridge
Dr. Christopher M. Span
Dr. William Sturkey
Various contemporary educators

NEWSPAPERS AND PERIODICALS

Association for the Study of African American Life and History (ASALH)
Hattiesburg, Mississippi Newspaper
History of Education Quarterly
The Journal of Negro History
Teachers in the Movement: Pedagogy, Activism, and Freedom—Derrick Alridge

COURT CASES

Brown v. Board of Education of Topeka, 347 U.S. 483 (1954)
Plessy v. Ferguson, 163 U.S. 537 (1896)

PUBLISHED WORKS

"About the Civil Rights Movement Archive." Accessed July 17, 2021. https://www.crmvet.org/about.htm.

Alridge, Derrick P., Jon N. Hale, and Tondra L. Loder-Jackson. *Schooling the Movement: The Activism of Southern Black Educators from Reconstruction through the Civil Rights Era*. Columbia: University of South Carolina Press, 2023.

Alridge, Derrick P. "The Dilemmas, Challenges, and Duality of an African-American Educational Historian." *Educational Researcher* 32, no. 9 (2003): 25–34.

———. "Teachers in the Civil Rights Movement: A UVA Oral-History Project." YouTube. University of Virginia, April 27, 2016. https://www.youtube.com/watch?v=xsegxK50xEU.

Anderson, James D. *The Education of Blacks in the South, 1860–1935*. Chapel Hill: University of North Carolina Press, 1988.

Anderson, James. "A Tale of Two *Browns*: Constitutional Equality and Unequal Education." *Yearbook of the National Society for the Study of Education* 105, no. 2 (2006): 14–35.

Anderson, Jessica Cumberbatch. "*Some of My Best Friends Are Black* Author

Bibliography

Says He Actually Had No Black Friends." HuffPost. July 25, 2012. https://www.huffpost.com/entry/tanner-colby-some-of-my-best-friends-are-black_n_1696145.

Appiah, K. A., and H. L. Gates Jr., eds. *Africana: The Encyclopedia of the African and African American Experience*. New York: Oxford University Press, 2005.

Apple, M. W. "The Absent Presence of Race in Educational Reform." *Race Ethnicity and Education* 2, no. 1 (1999): 9–16.

Aronowitz, Stanley, and Henry A. Giroux. *Education Still under Siege*. Westport, CT: Bergin and Garvey, 1994.

Aronson, Brittany, Lateasha Meyers, and Vanessa Winn. "'Lies My Teacher [Educator] Still Tells': Using Critical Race Counternarratives to Disrupt Whiteness in Teacher Education." *The Teacher Educator* 55, no. 3 (2020): 300–22. https://doi.org/10.1080/08878730.2020.1759743.

Ashford-Hanserd, Shetay, Stephen B. Springer, MaryPatricia Hayton, and Kelly E. Williams. "Shadows of Plessy v. Ferguson: The Dichotomy of Progress Toward Educational Equity Since 1954." *The Journal of Negro Education* 89, no. 4 (2020): 410–22.

"'Atlanta Compromise' Speech (18 September 1895)." *African American Studies Center*. 2009. https://doi.org/10.1093/acref/9780195301731.013.33544.

Baker, R. Scott. *Paradoxes of Desegregation: African American Struggles for Educational Equity in Charleston, South Carolina, 1926–1972*. Columbia: University of South Carolina, 2006.

Ball, Erica L. "Sarah's Long Walk: The Free Blacks of Boston and How Their Struggle for Equality Changed America." *The New England Quarterly* 79, no. 2 (2006): 331–33.

Ball, Eric L., and Alice Lai. Place-Based Pedagogy for the Arts and Humanities. *Pedagogy* 6, no. 2 (April 2006): 261–87.

Barnett, B. "Invisible Southern Black Women Leaders in the Civil Rights Movement: The Triple Constraints of Gender, Race, and Class." *Gender & Society* 7 (1993): 162–82.

Baumgartner, Kabria. "Building the Future: White Women, Black Education, and Civic Inclusion in Antebellum Ohio." *Journal of the Early Republic* 37, no. 1 (2017): 117–45.

Beauboeuf-Lafontant, Tamara. "A Womanist Experience of Caring: Understanding the Pedagogy of Exemplary Black Women Teachers." *The Urban Review* 34, no. 1 (2002): 71–86.

Bell, Derrick. "The Case for a Separate Black School System." In *Black Education: A Quest for Equity and Excellence*, edited by Willy DeMarcell Smith and Eva Wells Chunn, 137–46. New York: Routledge, 1989. https://doi.org/10.4324/9781351313841-13.

———. *Silent Covenants: Brown v. Board of Education and the Unfulfilled Hopes for Racial Reform*. Oxford: Oxford University Press, 2006.

———. *Faces at the Bottom of the Well: The Permanence of Racism*. New York: Basic Books, 2018.

Berrey, Stephen A. "Resistance Begins at Home: The Black Family and Lessons in Survival and Subversion in Jim Crow Mississippi." *Black Women, Gender & Families* 3, no. 1 (2009): 65–90. https://doi.org/10.1353/bwg.0.0000.

Bethune, Mary McLeod. "The Sacrifices and Achievements of African-American Women." *The Journal of Blacks in Higher Education*, no. 32 (2001): 35. https://doi.org/10.2307/2678758.

Bolton, Charles C. "The Last Stand of Massive Resistance: Mississippi Public School Integration, 1970." Mississippi History Now, 2000. http://www.mshistorynow.mdah.ms.gov/articles/305/the-last-stand-of-massive-resistance-1970.

———. "Mississippi's School Equalization Program, 1945–1954: 'A Last Gasp to Try to Maintain a Segregated Educational System.'" *The Journal of Southern History* 66, no. 4 (2000): 1, 2, 781–814. https://doi.org/10.2307/2588011.

Bond, Julian. "With All Deliberate Speed: *Brown vs. Board of Education*." *Indiana Law Journal* 90 (2015): 1671–81. https://doi.org/http://ilj.law.indiana.edu/articles/15-Bond.pdf.

———. "Julian Bond Oral History Project: Charlie Cobb." American University School of Public Affairs. YouTube video. April 8, 2019. https://youtu.be/P6D611NN07c.

Boustan, Leah Platt. "Black Migration from the South in Historical Context." In *Competition in the Promised Land: Black Migrants in Northern Cities and Labor Markets* 14–38. Princeton University Press, 2017. http://www.jstor.org/stable/j.ctt1q1xrc2.5.

Boyett, Patricia Michelle. "Race and Justice in Mississippi's Central Piney Woods, 1940–2010." Dissertation, University of Southern Mississippi, 2011.

Breathett, George. "Black Educators and the United States Supreme Court Decision of May 17, 1954 (*Brown versus the Board of Education*)." *The Journal of Negro History* 68, no. 2 (1983): 201–8. https://doi.org/10.2307/2717722.

Brown v. Board of Education of Topeka, Opinion. May 17, 1954. Records of the Supreme Court of the United States. Record Group 267. National Archives.

Buck, Stuart. *Acting White: The Ironic Legacy of Desegregation*. New Haven: Yale University Press, 2014.

Bunch, Lonnie. "Secretary Lonnie Bunch: It Is Time for America to Confront Its Tortured Racial Past." Smithsonian.com. Smithsonian Institution, May 31, 2020. https://www.smithsonianmag.com/smithsonian-institution/it-time-america-confront-its-tortured-racial-past-180975012/.

———. "Video: Keynote Speaker Lonnie Bunch, 2020 Asalh Black History Month Luncheon." ASALH. 2020. https://asalh.org/keynote-lonnie-bunch-2020-asalh-black-history-month-luncheon/.

Burrow, Rufus. "Mississippi: Made to Disappear." In *A Child Shall Lead Them: Martin Luther King Jr., Young People, and the Movement* 144–216. Minneapolis: Fortress Press. https://doi.org/10.2307/j.ctt9m0vcc.10.

Butchart, Ronald E. "Review of *The Education of Blacks in the South, 1860–1935*." *The American Historical Review* 95, no. 3 (1990): 915. https://doi.org/10.2307/2164473.

Bibliography

Camp, S. M. *Closer to Freedom*. Chapel Hill: University of North Carolina Press, 2004.

Card, Claudia, and Lorraine Code. "What Can She Know? Feminist Theory and the Construction of Knowledge." *The Philosophical Review* 101, no. 3 (1992): 662. https://doi.org/10.2307/2186072.

Carney, Leo. "The Vestiges of Jim Crow and the Mississippi Sovereignty Commission." Mississippi Free Press, June 12, 2024, https://www.mississippifreepress.org/the-vestiges-of-jim-crow-and-the-mississippi-sovereignty-commission/.

Cecelski, David. *Along Freedom Road*. Chapel Hill: University of North Carolina Press, 1994.

Center on Education Policy. "A Call to Action to Raise Achievement for African American Students." 2010. Retrieved from http://www.Cep-dc.org/displayDocument.cfm?DocumentID=111.

Championhilz. "'The First Fruits of a New System': Freedmen's Schools at Vicksburg." Mississippians in the Confederate Army. March 23, 2016. https://mississippiconfederates.wordpress.com/2016/03/23/the-first-fruits-of-anew-system-freedmens-schools-at-vicksburg/.

Chapman, Thandeka K. "Is Integration a Dream Deferred? Students of Color in Majority White Suburban Schools." *The Journal of Negro Education* 83, no. 3 (2014): 311–26. https://doi.org/10.7709/jnegroeducation.83.3.0311.

Charles Cobb, "Prospectus for a Summer Freedom School Program." Freedom School Curriculum. December 1963. http://www.educationanddemocracy.org/FSCfiles/B_05_ProspForFSchools.htm.

Charlton, Thomas L., Lois E. Myers, and Rebecca Sharpless. *History of Oral History: Foundations and Methodology*. Lanham, MD: Rowman and Littlefield, 2014.

Clark, Septima Poinsette, and Cynthia Stokes Brown. *Ready from Within: Septima Clark and the Civil Rights Movement*. Trenton, NJ: Africa World, 1996.

Clayton, Dewey M. "Black Lives Matter and the Civil Rights Movement: A Comparative Analysis of Two Social Movements in the United States." *Journal of Black Studies* 49, no. 5 (2018): 448–80.

Clemons, Kristal M. "I've Got to Do Something for My People: Black Women Teachers of the 1964 Mississippi Freedom Schools." *Western Journal of Black Studies* 38, no. 3 (2014): 141–54.

Collier-Thomas, Bettye, and V. P. Franklin. *Sisters in the Struggle: African American Women in the Civil Rights–Black Power Movement*. New York: New York University Press, 2001.

Collins, Patricia Hill. "The Politics of Black Feminist Thought." In Patricia Hill Collins, *Black Feminist Thought: Knowledge, Consciousness, and the Politics of Empowerment*. 2nd ed. 3–27. New York: Routledge, 1990, 2000, 2022. https://doi.org/10.4324/9781003245650-2.

"The Complete Bibliography of *The Journal of Negro Education*, 1932–2006." *The Journal of Negro Education* 75, no. 2 (2006): 73–318.

Cozart, S., and P. Groves-Price. "Black Women, Identity, and Schooling:

Reclaiming Our Work in Shifting Context." *The Urban Review* 37, no. 3 (2005): 173–79.

Crawford, V., J. Rouse, and B. Woods. *Women in the Civil Rights Movement.* Bloomington: Indiana University Press, 1993.

Crenshaw, K. G. *Critical Race Theory: The Key Writings That Formed the Movement.* New York: The New Press, 1995.

Crenshaw, K. W. "Mapping the Margins: Intersectionality, Identity Politics, and Violence against Women of Color." *Stanford Law Review* 43, no. 6 (1991): 1241–99.

———. "Demarginalizing the Intersections of Race and Sex: A Black Feminist Critique of Antidiscrimination Doctrine, Feminist Theory, and Antiracist Politics." In *Critical Race Feminism,* edited by A. K. Wing, 23–33. New York: New York University Press, 2003.

Creswell, John W., and Cheryl N. Poth. *Qualitative Inquiry and Research Design: Choosing among Five Approaches.* Thousand Oaks, CA: SAGE, 2018.

Crosby, Emilye. "Glenda Funchess Oral History Interview Conducted by Emilye Crosby in Hattiesburg, Mississippi, December 2, 2015." The Library of Congress. December 2, 2015. https://www.loc.gov/item/2016655407/.

Dahmer, Vernon. "Black Community Leader Killed in Klan Bombing, Hattiesburg, Miss., 1966." *Chicago Tribune (1963–1996),* November 5, 1989. https://www.proquest.com/historical-newspapers/black-community-leader-killed-klan-bombing/docview/1019121924/se-2?accountid=14553.

Daly, A., J. Jennings, J. O. Beckett, and B. R. Leashore. "Effective Coping Strategies of African Americans." *Social Work* 40, no. 2 (1995): 240–48.

Daugherity, Brian J., and Brian Grogan, eds. "'Massive Resistance.'" In *A Little Child Shall Lead Them: A Documentary Account of the Struggle for School Desegregation in Prince Edward County, Virginia* 80–111. University of Virginia Press, 2019. https://doi.org/10.2307/j.ctvndv7vw.10.

Davis, Angela Yvonne. *Women, Race and Class.* New York: Vintage Books, 1994.

Delpit, L. "The Silenced Dialogue: Power and Pedagogy in Educating Other People's Children." *Harvard Educational Review* 58, no. 3 (1988): 280–98.

Dewey, John. "My Pedagogic Creed." *Exploring Education* (2017): 215–18. https://doi.org/10.4324/9781315408545-13.

Dingfelder, S. "African American Women at Risk." *Monitor on Psychology* 44, no. 1 (2013): 56.

Dittmer, John. *Local People: The Struggle for Civil Rights in Mississippi.* Urbana: University of Illinois Press, 2006.

Division of Administration and Finance. *Biennial Report and Recommendations of the State Superintendent of Public Education, Scholastic Years 1953–1954 and 1954–1955.* Jackson, MS: State Government Printing Office, 1956.

Dougherty, Jack. "From Anecdote to Analysis: Oral Interviews and New Scholarship in Educational History." *The Journal of American History* 86, no. 2 (1999): 712–23. https://doi.org/10.2307/2567055.

Douglass, Frederick. *The Life and Times of Frederick Douglass*. Hartford, CT: Park Publishing Company, 1892.

Du Bois, W. E. B., ed. *The Negro Common School (Atlanta University Study Number 6)*. New York: Arno Press, 1901.

Du Bois, W. E. B. "Does the Negro Need Separate Schools?" *The Journal of Negro Education* 4, no. 3 (1935): 328–35. https://doi.org/10.2307/2291871.

Ethridge, Samuel B. "Impact of the 1954 Brown vs. Topeka Board of Education Decision on Black Educators." *The Negro Educational Review* 30, no. 4 (2001): 219–22. https://www.proquest.com/scholarly-journals/impact-1954-brown-vs-topeka-board-education/docview/1304522721/se-2.

Ewing, Eve L. *Ghosts in the Schoolyard: Racism and School Closings on Chicago's South Side*. Chicago: University of Chicago Press, 2020.

Fairclough, Adam. "'Being in the Field of Education and Also Being a Negro . . . Seems . . . Tragic': Black Teachers in the Jim Crow South." *Journal of American History* 87, no. 1 (2000): 65–97. https://doi.org/10.2307/2567916.

———. *Teaching Equality: Black Schools in the Age of Jim Crow*. Athens: University of Georgia Press, 2001.

———. "The Costs of *Brown*: Black Teachers and School Integration." *Journal of American History* 91, no. 1 (2004): 43–55. https://doi.org/10.2307/3659612.

———. *A Class of Their Own: Black Teachers in the Segregated South*. England: Belknap Press of Harvard University Press, 2007.

Ficker, Douglas J. "From *Roberts* to *Plessy*: Educational Segregation and the 'Separate but Equal' Doctrine." *The Journal of Negro History* 84, no. 4 (1999): 301–14. https://doi.org/10.2307/2649034.

Fields, Liz. "The Story behind Nina Simone's Protest Song, 'Mississippi Goddam.'" PBS. Public Broadcasting Service, June 21, 2022. https://www.pbs.org/wnet/americanmasters/the-story-behind-nina-simones-protest-song-mississippi-goddam/16651/.

FORDETRA Reunion Book. Hattiesburg, Mississippi: July 2010.

Foner, Eric. *Nothing But Freedom: Emancipation and Its Legacy*. Baton Rouge: Louisiana State University Press, 2011.

Ford, Tanisha C. "SNCC's Soul Sisters." In *Liberated Threads: Black Women, Style, and the Global Politics of Soul* 67–93. Chapel Hill: University of North Carolina Press, 2015.

Foster, M. "The Politics of Race: Through the Eyes of African-American Teachers." *Journal of Education* 172 (1990): 123–41.

———. "African-American Teachers and Culturally Relevant Pedagogy." In *Handbook of Research on Multicultural Education*, edited by J. Banks, 570–87. New York: Simon and Schuster, 1995.

———. *Black Teachers on Teaching*. New York: The New Press, 1997.

Frankenberg, Erica. "70 Years after Brown vs. Board of Education, Public Schools Still Deeply Segregated." The Conversation, January 5, 2024. https://theconversation.com/70-years-after-brown-vs-board-of-education-public

-schools-still-deeply-segregated-219654?utm_medium=email&utm_
campaign=Daily%20Newsletter%20%20January%205%202024%20-%20
2842228811&utm_content=Daily%20Newsletter%20%20January%20
5%202024%20-%202842228811+CID_ee8ad5dcf03782f173d6f7b7aabfdff
7&utm_source=campaign_monitor_us&utm_term=Public%20schools%20
still%20segregated%2070%20years%.

Franklin, John Hope, and Evelyn Brooks Higginbotham. *From Slavery to Freedom: A History of African Americans*. New York: McGraw-Hill, 2021.

Franklin, V. P. "Review of *Whatever Happened to the College-Bred Negro?* by Clayborne Carson and Gail E. Thomas." *History of Education Quarterly* 24, no. 3 (1984): 411–18. https://doi.org/10.2307/368016.

———. "'Voice of the Black Community': *The Philadelphia Tribune*, 1912–41." *Pennsylvania History: A Journal of MidAtlantic Studies* 51, no. 4 (1984): 261–84.

———. "Reflections on History, Education, and Social Theories." *History of Education Quarterly* 51, no. 2 (2011): 264–71.

Fredrickson, George M., and Albert Camarillo. *Racism: A Short History*. Princeton: Princeton University Press, 2015.

Frey, William H. "The New Great Migration: Black Americans' Return to the South, 1965–2000." In *Redefining Urban and Suburban America: Evidence from Census 2000*, edited by Alan Berube, Bruce Katz, and Robert E. Lang, 87–110. Brookings Institution Press, 2005.

Fultz, Michael. "African-American Teachers in the South, 1890–1940: Growth, Feminization, and Salary Discrimination." *Teachers College Record: The Voice of Scholarship in Education* 96, no. 3 (1995): 1–25. https://doi.org/10.1177/016146819509600312.

———. "African American Teachers in the South, 1890–1940: Powerlessness and the Ironies of Expectations and Protest." *History of Education Quarterly* 35, no. 4 (1995): 401–22. https://doi.org/10.2307/369578.

———. "Teacher Training and African American Education in the South, 1900–1940." *The Journal of Negro Education* 64, no. 2 (1995): 196–210. https://doi.org/10.2307/2967242.

———. "The Displacement of Black Educators Post-*Brown*: An Overview and Analysis." *History of Education Quarterly* 44, no. 1 (2004): 11–45.

Funchess, Glenda. "Hattiesburg Schools Desegregation Took 10 Years." *Hattiesburg American*. September 18, 2015. https://www.hattiesburgamerican.com/story/opinion/columnists/2015/09/18/fiftieth-anniversary-hattiesburg-desegregation/32551069/.

Fuquay, Michael W. "Civil Rights and the Private School Movement in Mississippi, 1964–1971." *History of Education Quarterly* 42, no. 2 (2002): 159–80. https://doi.org/10.1111/j.1748-5959.2002.tb00105.x.

Gaertner, S. L., and J. F. Dovidio. *The Aversive Form of Racism*. Academic Press, 1986.

Bibliography

Gaines, Doris Townsend, and Carolyn Abrams. *The Class of 1968: A Thread through Time.* Conneaut Lake, PA: Page Publishing, Inc., 2021.

Gaspar, D. B., and D. C. Hine. *More Than Chattel: Black Women and Slavery in the Americas.* Bloomington: Indiana University Press, 1996.

Gavins, Raymond. "Literature on Jim Crow." *OAH Magazine of History* 18, no. 2 (2004): 13–14. http://www.jstor.org/stable/25163655.

Giddings, P. *When and Where I Enter: The Impact of Black Women on Race and Sex in America.* New York: Bantam, 1984.

Gilbert, P., N. LeBrun, A. D. Singer, and T. Walker, producers, and Gilbert, P., director. *With All Deliberate Speed.* Motion picture. Discovery Docs. 2004.

Giroux, H. A. "Obama's Dilemma: Post Partisan Politics and the Crisis of American Education." *Harvard Educational Review* 79, no. 2 (2009): 250–66.

Givens, Jarvis R. *Fugitive Pedagogy: Carter G. Woodson and the Art of Black Teaching.* Cambridge: Harvard University Press, 2021.

———. "What's Missing from the Discourse about Anti-Racist Teaching." *The Atlantic.* May 21, 2021. https://www.theatlantic.com/ideas/archive/2021/05/whats-missing-from-the-discourse-about-anti-racist-teaching/618947/.

Glassie, Henry. "The Practice and Purpose of History." *The Journal of American History* 81, no. 3 (1994): 966. https://doi.org/10.2307/2081435.

Goertzen, Chris. "Freedom Songs: Helping Black Activists, Black Residents, and White Volunteers Work Together in Hattiesburg, Mississippi, during the Summer of 1964." *Black Music Research Journal* 36, no. 1 (2016): 59–85. https://doi.org/10.5406/blacmusiresej.36.1.0059.

Goodwin, A. L. "Historical and Contemporary Perspectives on Multicultural Teacher Education." In *Preparing Teachers for Cultural Diversity*, edited by J. King, E. Hollins, and W. Hayman, 5–22. New York: Teachers College Press, 1997.

Goodwine, Marquetta L. "The Legacy of Ibo Landing." Smithsonian Libraries. July 16, 2019. https://library.si.edu/donate/adopt-a-book/legacy-ibo-landing.

Google. "Climatological Data." Google Books. Accessed August 1, 2021. https://books.google.com/books?id=LhKgif_dBVYC&pg=RA4-PA18&lpg=RA4-PA18&dq=the%2Bleaf%2Briver%2Bflood%2Bof%2B1974&source=bl&ots=V47BqqNq5M&sig=BB61vLacpiOg3Yef6c5ZmjwrfH4&hl=en&sa=X&ei=W9zrUsOaDY6vsQTs9IDABQ&ved=0CFcQ6AewBw#v=onepage&q=the%20leaf%20river%20flood%20of%201974&f=false.

Gordon, J. A. "Why Students of Color Are Not Entering Teaching: Reflections from Minority Teachers." *Journal of Teacher Education* 45, no. 5 (1994): 346–53.

———. *The Color of Teaching.* New York: Routledge Falmer, 2000.

"Great Migration Initiative: Mississippi Department of Archives & History." Mississippi Department of Archives & History, 2022. https://www.mdah.ms.gov/greatmigration.

Grove, Garret. "Mississippi Has 30 School Districts with Desegregation Orders: DOJ, May 29, 2024. https://www.wjtv.com/news/education/mississippi-has-30-school-districts-with-desegregation-orders-doj/.

Hale, Jon N. *A History of the Mississippi Freedom Schools, 1954–1965*. Urbana: University of Illinois Press, 2009.

———. "'The Student as a Force for Social Change': The Mississippi Freedom Schools and Student Engagement." *The Journal of African American History* 96, no. 3 (2011): 325–47. https://doi.org/10.5323/jafriamerhist.96.3.0325.

———. *The Freedom Schools: Student Activists in the Mississippi Civil Rights Movement*. New York: Columbia University Press, 2018.

———. "'The Development of Power Is the Main Business of the School': The Agency of Southern Black Teacher Associations from Jim Crow through Desegregation." *The Journal of Negro Education* 87, no. 4 (2018): 444–59. https://doi.org/10.7709/jnegroeducation.87.4.0444.

———. "'We Are Not Merging on an Equal Basis': The Desegregation of Southern Teacher Associations and the Right to Work, 1945–1977." *Labor History* 60, no. 5 (December 2019): 463–81.

Haney, James E. "The Effects of the *Brown* Decision on Black Educators." *The Journal of Negro Education* 47, no. 1 (1978): 88–95. https://doi.org/10.2307/2967104.

Hannah-Jones, Nikole. "Our Democracy's Founding Ideals Were False When They Were Written. Black Americans Have Fought to Make Them True." *The Best American Magazine Writing 2020*, 2021, 359–82. https://doi.org/10.7312/holt19801-018.

Harrison, R. K. *Enslaved Women and the Art of Resistance in Antebellum America*. New York: Palgrave Macmillan, 2009.

Hartman, Saidiya. *Lose Your Mother*. New York: Farrar, Straus and Giroux, 2008.

Hattiesburg American. "16 Negro First-Graders Quietly Begin Mixed Classes in Biloxi." September 3, 1966.

Hawkins, David. *The Informed Vision Essays on Learning and Human Nature*. New York: Algora Publishing, 2007.

Heller, Rafael. "Telling the Untold Stories of School Integration: An Interview with Vanessa Siddle Walker." *Phi Delta Kappan* 100, no. 5 (2019): 43–49. https://doi.org/10.1177/0031721719827546.

Henry, A. "Complacent and Womanish: Girls Negotiating Their Lives in an African Centered School in the U.S." *Race, Ethnicity and Education* 1, no. 2 (1998): 151–70.

Hine, Darlene Clark. *Hine Sight: Black Women and the Re-Construction of American History*. Bloomington: Indiana University Press, 1998.

———. "Black Professionals and Race Consciousness: Origins of the Civil Rights Movement, 1890–1950." *The Journal of American History* 89, no. 4 (2003): 1279–94. https://doi.org/10.2307/3092543.

———. "African American Women and Their Communities in the Twentieth Century: The Foundation and Future of Black Women's Studies." *Black Women, Gender + Families* 1, no. 1 (2007): 1–23.

Hines, Erica, and Michael Hines. "Black Teachers Are Critical to the Success of Black Students." *Time*. August 11, 2020. https://time.com/5876164/black-teachers/.

Holsaert, Faith S., Martha P. Noonan, Judy Richardson, Betty Garman Robinson, Jean Smith Young, and Dorothy Zellner. *Hands on the Freedom Plow: Personal Accounts by Women in SNCC*. Urbana: University of Illinois Press, 2012.

Hooker, Robert W. *Displacement of Black Teachers in the Eleven Southern States. Special Report*. Ann Arbor: University of Michigan Press. ERIC. November 30, 1970. https://eric.ed.gov/?id=ED047036.

Houck, Davis W. "Killing Emmett." *Rhetoric & Public Affairs* 8, no. 2 (2005): 1.

"How Desegregation Changed Us: The Effects of Racially Mixed Schools on Students and Society." Teachers College, Columbia University. October 14, 2004. https://www.tc.columbia.edu/articles/2004/march/how-desegregation-changed-us-the-effects-of-racially-mixed-/.

Howard-Baptiste, S., and J. C. Harris. Teaching Then and Now: Black Female Scholars and the Mission to Move beyond Border. *Negro Educational Review* 65, no. 1–4 (2014): 5–22.

Howard-Vital, Michelle R., and Jacqueline Jordan Irvine. "Black Students and School Failure: Policies, Practices, and Prescriptions." *The Journal of Negro Education* 60, no. 2 (1991): 229–30. https://doi.org/10.2307/2295613.

Hudson, Mildred J., and Barbara J. Holmes. "Missing Teachers, Impaired Communities: The Unanticipated Consequences of Brown v. Board of Education on the African American Teaching Force at the Precollegiate Level." *The Journal of Negro Education* 63, no. 3 (1994): 388–93. https://doi.org/10.2307/2967189.

Hurston, Zora Neale. *Barracoon: The Story of the Last "Black Cargo."* London: HQ, 2018.

Hyland, Nora E. "Being a Good Teacher of Black Students? White Teachers and Unintentional Racism." *Curriculum Inquiry* 35, no. 4 (2005): 429–59.

Ida B. Wells Memorial Foundation. "Protect, Preserve, Promote the Legacy of Ida B. Wells." 2021. https://ibwfoundation.org/.

Irons, Peter H. *Jim Crow's Children: The Broken Promise of the Brown Decision*. New York: Penguin Books, 2004.

Irvine, Jacqueline Jordan. "An Analysis of the Problem of Disappearing Black Educators." *The Elementary School Journal* 88, no. 5 (1988): 503–13. https://doi.org/10.1086/461553.

Irvine, R. W., and Irvine, J. J. "The Impact of the Desegregation Process on the Education of Black Students: Key Variables." *The Journal of Negro Education* 52, 410–22 (1983). https://doi.org/10.2307/2294948.

Irvine, J. J., and R. W. Irvine. "The Impact of the Desegregation Process on the Education of Black Students: A Retrospective Analysis." *The Journal of Negro Education* 76, no. 3 (2007): 297–305. http://www.jstor.org/stable/40034572.

Jackson, Errin. "Nannie Helen Burroughs (1883–1961)." The Library of Congress. August 8, 2019. https://www.blackpast.org/african-american-history/burroughs-nannie-helen-1883-1961/.

Jeffries, R. "Editor's Introduction: Fortitudinous Femininity: Black Women's Resilience in the Face of Struggle." *Western Journal of Black Studies* 39, no. 2 (2015): 81–83.

Johnston, E. "Attitudes in Mississippi." Civil Rights Digital Library, December 1967. https://usm.access.preservica.com/uncategorized/IO_34c1b8a8-da4d-4648-948b-452763773de5.

Jones, C., and K. Shorter-Gooden. *Shifting: The Double Lives of Black Women in America*. New York: Harper, 2003.

Jones, Susan R. "Constructing Identities at the Intersections: An Autoethnographic Exploration of Multiple Dimensions of Identity." *Journal of College Student Development* 50, no. 3 (2009): 287–304. https://doi.org/10.1353/csd.0.0070.

Jordan-Taylor, Donna J. "'I'm Not Autherine Lucy': The Circular Migration of Southern Black Professionals Who Completed Graduate School in the North during Jim Crow, 1945–1970." Dissertation, University of Washington, 2011.

Kasher, Steven, and Myrlie Evers-Williams. "The Civil Rights Movement: A Photographic History, 1954–68." Amazon. Abbeville Press, 2000. https://www.amazon.com/Civil-Rights-Movement-Photographic-History/dp/0789206560.

Kelley, Robin D. G. "'We Are Not What We Seem': Rethinking Black Working-Class Opposition in the Jim Crow South." *The Journal of American History* 80, no. 1 (1993): 75–112. https://doi.org/10.2307/2079698.

Kendrick, Paul, and Stephen Kendrick. "Sarah's Long Walk: The Free Blacks of Boston and How Their Struggle for Equality Changed America." *Choice Reviews Online* 43, no. 4 (2005): 330–33. https://doi.org/10.5860/choice.43-2423.

Ketelle, Diane. "Introduction to the Special Issue: What Is Storytelling in the Higher Education Classroom?" *Storytelling, Self, Society* 13, no. 2 (2017): 143–50. https://doi.org/10.13110/storselfsoci.13.2.0143.

King, Joyce Elaine, Etta R. Hollins, and Warren C. Hayman. *Preparing Teachers for Cultural Diversity*. New York: Teachers College Press, 1997.

Kluger, Richard. *Simple Justice: The History of Brown v. Board of Education and Black America's Struggle for Equality*. New York: Vintage Books, 2004.

Ladner, Joyce A. *Tomorrow's Tomorrow: The Black Woman*. Lincoln: University of Nebraska Press, 1995.

———. *The Ties That Bind: Timeless Values for African American Families*. Chichester, NH: Wiley, 2000.

———. "A New Civil Rights Agenda." *The Brookings Review* 18, no. 2 (2000): 26–28. https://doi.org/10.2307/20080906.

———. "Mississippi Movement Set Example for Female Leaders." *Clarion Ledger*. June 27, 2014. https://www.clarionledger.com/story/journey tojustice/2014/06/27/mississippi-movement-female-leaders/11446273/.

———. "Joyce Ladner Interview for Julian Bond Oral History Project." Vimeo. Julian Bond Oral History Project, July 5, 2022. https://vimeo.com/696644718.

Ladson-Billings, Gloria. "Toward a Theory of Culturally Relevant Pedagogy." *American Educational Research Journal* 32, no. 3 (1995): 465–91.

———. "New Directions in Multicultural Education: Complexities, Boundaries, and Critical Race Theory." In *Handbook of Research on Multicultural Education*, 2nd ed., edited by J. A. Banks and C. A. McGee Banks, 50–68. New York: Jossey Bass, 2003.

———. "Foreword." In *Black Education: A Transformative Research and Action Agenda for the New Century*, edited by J. King, xiii–xvii. New Jersey: Erlbaum Press, 2005.

———. *The Dream Keepers: Successful Teachers of African American Children*. 2nd ed. San Francisco: Jossey-Bass, 2009.

———. "Race . . . to the Top, Again: Comments on the Genealogy of Critical Race Theory." *Connecticut Law Review* 43, no. 5 (2011): 1439–57.

———. "Through a Glass Darkly: The Persistence of Race in Education Research and Scholarship." *Educational Researcher* 41, no. 4 (2012): 115–20. https://doi.org/10.3102/0013189X12440743.

Lafontant, Tamara Beauboeuf. "A Womanist Experience of Caring: Understanding the Pedagogy of Exemplary Black Women Teachers." *The Urban Review* (2002). https://link.springer.com/content/pdf/10.1023%2FA%3A1014497228517.pdf.

Lash, Martha, and Monica Ratcliffe. "The Journey of an African American Teacher before and after Brown v. Board of Education." *The Journal of Negro Education* 83, no. 3 (2014): 327–37. https://doi.org/10.7709/jnegroeducation.83.3.0327.

Lawson, Erica. "Bereaved Black Mothers and Maternal Activism in the Racial State." *Feminist Studies* 44, no. 3 (2018): 713–35. https://doi.org/10.15767/feministstudies.44.3.0713.

Lerner, Gerda. *Black Women in White America: A Documentary History*. New York: Vintage Books, 1992.

Lewis, Amanda E. "There Is No 'Race' in the Schoolyard: Color-Blind Ideology in an (Almost) All-White School." *American Educational Research Journal* 38, no. 4 (2001): 781–811.

Lipsitz, George. *The Possessive Investment in Whiteness*. Philadelphia: Temple University Press, 2018.

Lomotey, Kofi. *Encyclopedia of African American Education*. Los Angeles: SAGE, 2010.

Love, Bettina L. "Anti-Black State Violence, Classroom Edition: The Spirit Murdering of Black Children." *Journal of Curriculum and Pedagogy* 13, no. 1 (2016): 22–25. https://doi.org/10.1080/15505170.2016.1138258.

———. *We Want to Do More than Survive: Abolitionist Teaching and the Pursuit of Educational Freedom*. Boston: Beacon Press, 2020.

Lutz, Mallory. "The Hidden Cost of Brown v. Board: African American Educators' Resistance to Desegregating Schools." *Online Journal of Rural Research & Policy* 12, no. 4 (2017): 1–29. https://doi.org/10.4148/1936-0487.1085.

Madkins, Tia C. "The Black Teacher Shortage: A Literature Review of Historical and Contemporary Trends." *The Journal of Negro Education* 80 (2011): 417–27. http://www.jstor.org/stable/41341143.

Malone, Bill C., Guy Carawan, Candie Carawan, Pete Seeger, and Bob Reiser. "Sing for Freedom: The Story of the Civil Rights Movement Through Its Songs." *The Journal of Southern History* 59, no. 1 (1993): 175–93. https://doi.org/10.2307/2210403.

Marck, Jason. "Dr. Lonnie Bunch Preserves History Memory and the African American Experience." WBEZ Chicago. WBEZ Chicago, June 27, 2017. https://www.wbez.org/stories/dr-lonnie-bunch-preserves-history-memory-and-the-african-american-experience/1727f361-c699-4422-bd59-0489ce47ffb7.

Marcucci, Olivia. "Zora Neale Hurston and the *Brown* Debate: Race, Class, and the Progressive Empire." *The Journal of Negro Education* 86, no. 1 (2017): 13–24. https://doi.org/10.7709/jnegroeducation.86.1.0013.

Margo, Robert A. *Race and Schooling in the South, 1880–1950: An Economic History*. Chicago: University of Chicago Press, 1990.

Mayes, Edward. *History of Education in Mississippi* (version aen6226.0001.001.umich.edu). Internet Archive. Washington: United States Government, 1899. https://archive.org/details/aen6226.0001.001.umich.edu/page/n1/mode/2up.

McGrady, Patrick B., and John R. Reynolds. "Racial Mismatch in the Classroom." *Sociology of Education* 86, no. 1 (2012): 3–17. https://doi.org/10.1177/0038040712444857.

McLemore, Richard Aubrey. *A History of Mississippi*. Hattiesburg: University and College Press of Mississippi, 1973.

McMillen, Neil R. *The Citizens Council: A History of Organized Southern White Resistance to the Second Reconstruction*. Urbana: University of Illinois Press, 1971.

———. *The Citizens' Council: Organized Resistance to the Second Reconstruction, 1954–64*. Urbana: University of Illinois Press, 1994.

———. *Dark Journey: Black Mississippians in the Age of Jim Crow*. New York: ACLS History E-Book Project, 2005.

Milner, H. Richard. "The Promise of Black Teachers' Success with Black Students." *Educational Foundations* 20 (2006): 89–104. https://files.eric.ed.gov/fulltext/EJ794734.pdf.

Bibliography

Milner, H. Richard, and Tyrone C. Howard. "Black Teachers, Black Students, Black Communities, and Brown: Perspectives and Insights from Experts." *The Journal of Negro Education* 73, no. 3 (2004): 285–97. https://doi.org/10.2307/4129612.

Mirza, H. "Plotting a History: Black and Colonial Feminisms in 'New Times.'" *Race, Ethnicity, and Education* 12, no. 1 (2009): 1–10.

"Mississippi's Broken Education Promise—A Timeline." Southern Poverty Law Center, May 23, 2017. https://www.splcenter.org/20170523/mississippi%E2%80%99s-broken-education-promise-%E2%80%93-timeline.

"Mississippi Statistical Abstract, State College." Division of Research, College of Business and Industry, Mississippi State University, 1970.

Morgan, Jennifer. "Laboring Women: Reproduction and Gender in New World Slavery (Early American Studies)," 2004. https://redrockweb.co/Laboring-Women:-Reproduction-And-Gender-In-New-World-Slavery-(Early-American-Studies)%7CJennifer-L.-Morgan.htm15.

Morris, Tiyi M. *Womanpower Unlimited and the Black Freedom Struggle in Mississippi*. Athens: University of Georgia Press, 2015.

Morris, Vivian Gunn, and Curtis L. Morris. *The Price They Paid: Desegregation in an African American Community*. New York: Teachers College Press, 2002.

Mosnier, Joseph. "Dorie Ann Ladner and Joyce Ladner Oral History Interview Conducted by Joseph Mosnier in Washington, DC, September 20, 2011." The Library of Congress. Civil Rights History Project Collection, September 20, 2011. https://www.loc.gov/item/2015669153/.

Moss, Hilary J. "The Tarring and Feathering of Thomas Paul Smith: Common Schools, Revolutionary Memory, and the Crisis of Black Citizenship in Antebellum Boston." *The New England Quarterly* 80, no. 2 (2007): 218–41. https://doi.org/10.1162/tneq.2007.80.2.218.

Nasstrom, Kathryn L. "Between Memory and History: Autobiographies of the Civil Rights Movement and the Writing of Civil Rights History." *The Journal of Southern History* 74, no. 2 (2008): 325–64. http://www.jstor.org/stable/27650145.

National Center for Education Statistics (NCES). "Digest of Education Statistics (NCES 2010–013)." Washington, DC: 2010.

Nave, R. L. "Mississippi Still Has Worst Poverty, Household Income." *Mississippi Today*, May 10, 2021. https://mississippitoday.org/2017/09/14/mississippi-still-worst-poverty-household-income-us/.

Noonan, Martha. "Martha Prescod Norman Noonan Oral History Interview Conducted by John Dittmer in Cockeysville, Maryland, March 18, 2013." The Library of Congress. Smithsonian, March 18, 2013. https://www.loc.gov/item/2015669179/.

O'Connor, Len. "Malcolm X Interview, 1963 Chicago." Facebook. September 29, 2019. https://www.facebook.com/watch/?ref=search&v=1047543662082637&external_log_id=c6b68252-bd8b-412d-96d9-2a93d2c28458&q=ississ%20x%20interview.

Olsen, Otto H. "Review of *Nothing but Freedom: Emancipation and Its Legacy*, by E. Foner." *Science & Society* 49, no. 2 (1985): 251–54. http://www.jstor.org/stable/40402657.

Onwuachi-Willig, Angela. "Reconceptualizing the Harms of Discrimination: How *Brown v. Board of Education* Helped to Further White Supremacy." *Virginia Law Review* 105, no. 2 (2019): 343–69. https://www.jstor.org/stable/26842241.

Orfield, Gary, Christine Mattise, Brian Willoughby. "*Brown v. Board*: Timeline of School Integration in the U.S." Learning for Justice. 2004. https://www.learningforjustice.org/magazine/spring-2004/brown-v-board-timeline-of-school-integration-in-the-us.

Parker, Nakia D. "Black Codes and Slave Codes." *African American Studies*, 2020. https://doi.org/10.1093/obo/9780190280024-0083.

Patton, John Leslie. "Reflections on Cultural Conflicts in the South." *Journal of Educational Sociology* 13, no. 9 (1940): 515–24. https://doi.org/10.2307/2261715.

Payne, Charles M. "'The Whole United States Is Southern!': *Brown v. Board* and the Mystification of Race." *Journal of American History* 91, no. 1 (2004): 83–91. https://doi.org/10.2307/3659615.

———. *I've Got the Light of Freedom: The Organizing Tradition and the Mississippi Freedom Struggle*, 2nd ed. Berkeley: University of California Press, 2007.

———. "Testing the Limits: Black Activism in Postwar Mississippi." In *I've Got the Light of Freedom: The Organizing Tradition and the Mississippi Freedom Struggle, With a New Preface*, 2nd ed., 29–66. Berkeley: University of California Press, 2007.

Perkins, Alfred. "Welcome Consequences and Fulfilled Promise: Julius Rosenwald Fellows and '*Brown v. Board of Education*.'" *The Journal of Negro Education* 72, no. 3 (2003): 344–56. https://doi.org/10.2307/3211252.

Perkins, Linda M. "The Racial Integration of the Seven Sister Colleges." *The Journal of Blacks in Higher Education*, no. 19 (1998): 104–8. https://doi.org/10.2307/2998936.

———. "'Bound to Them by a Common Sorrow': African American Women, Higher Education, and Collective Advancement." *The Journal of African American History* 100, no. 4 (2015): 721–47. https://doi.org/10.5323/jafriamerhist.100.4.0721.

Perlstein, Daniel. "Teaching Freedom: SNCC and the Creation of the Mississippi Freedom Schools." *History of Education Quarterly* 30, no. 3 (1990): 297–324. https://doi.org/10.2307/368691.

Perry, Andre. "The Educational Value of a Black Teacher." The Hechinger Report. October 21, 2020. https://hechingerreport.org/the-educational-value-of-a-black-teacher/.

Perry, Thelma D. *History of the American Teachers Association*. Washington, DC: National Education Association, 1995.

Pinar, William F. "Black Protest and the Emergence of Ida B. Wells." *Counterpoints* 163 (2001): 419–86.

Pinder, P. J. "The 'Black Girl Turn' in Research on Gender and Science Education: Toward Exploring and Understanding the Early Experiences of Black Females." 2008. Retrieved from ERIC database (ED499925).

Portelli, Alessandro. *The Battle of Valle Giulia: Oral History and the Art of Dialogue.* Madison: University of Wisconsin Press, 1997.

———. "What Makes Oral History Different." In Robert Perks, Alistair Thomson, Alex Haley, Alessandro Portelli, and Graham Smith, *The Oral History Reader*, 3rd ed., 52. London: Routledge/Taylor and Francis Group, 2016.

Rabinowitz, Tamar. "Teaching Women's History: Women of the Great Migration." New York Historical Society Museum and Library. June 27, 2018. https://womenatthecenter.nyhistory.org/women-of-the-great-migration/.

Rasmussen, Birgit Brander. "'Attended with Great Inconveniences': Slave Literacy and the 1740 South Carolina Negro Act." *PMLA* 125, no. 1 (2010): 201–3. http://www.jstor.org/stable/25614450.

Read, Frank T., and Lucy S. McGough. *Let Them Be Judged: The Judicial Integration of the Deep South.* Metuchen, NJ: Scarecrow Press, 1978.

Reber, S. J. "School Desegregation and Educational Attainment for Blacks." *Journal of Human Resources* 45 (2010): 893–914.

———. "From Separate and Unequal to Integrated and Equal? School Desegregation and School Finance in Louisiana." *The Review of Economics and Statistics* 93 (2011): 404–15.

Richardson, David. "Shipboard Revolts, African Authority, and the Atlantic Slave Trade." *The William and Mary Quarterly* 58, no. 1 (2001): 69–92. https://doi.org/10.2307/2674419.

Richmond, Emily. "Schools Are More Segregated Today Than During the Late 1960s." *The Atlantic.* Atlantic Media Company, June 11, 2012. https://www.theatlantic.com/national/archive/2012/06/schools-are-more-segregated-today-than-during-the-late-1960s/258348/.

Rizga, Kristina. "What If Teachers Didn't Focus So Much on Individual Achievement?" *The Atlantic.* September 9, 2020. https://www.theatlantic.com/education/archive/2019/06/how-black-teachers-segregated-district-teach-civics/591856/.

Rogers, Kim Lacy. "Oral History and the History of the Civil Rights Movement." *The Journal of American History* 75, no. 2 (1988): 567–76. https://doi.org/10.2307/1887873.

Rousmaniere, Kate. "Those Who Can't, Teach: The Disabling History of American Educators." *History of Education Quarterly* 53, no. 1 (2013): 90–103. https://doi.org/10.1111/hoeq.12004.

Russo, Charles J., J. John Harris, and Rosetta F. Sandidge. "*Brown v. Board of Education* at 40: A Legal History of Equal Educational Opportunities in American Public Education." *The Journal of Negro Education* 63, no. 3 (1994): 297–309. https://doi.org/10.2307/2967182.

Sack, Kevin. "Mississippi Reveals Dark Secrets of a Racist Time." *New York Times*. March 18, 1998. https://www.nytimes.com/1998/03/18/us/mississippi-reveals-dark-secrets-of-a-racist-time.html.

Saias, Brooke. "Explainer: Why Is America's Teaching Force So White?" *Education Week*. December 7, 2021. https://www.edweek.org/teaching-learning/video-explainer-why-is-americas-teaching-force-so-white/2021/12.

Sass, Herbert Ravenal. "Mixed Schools and Mixed Blood; 1956." Digital Collections at the University of Southern Mississippi. Accessed September 7, 2022. https://usm.access.preservica.com/uncategorized/IO_e65c4a3a-f86d-4ad7-9738-4f55e17ba806/.

"Separate But Not Equal: The Stories Behind *Brown v. Board of Education*." YouTube. March 28, 2020. https://www.youtube.com/watch?v=a-hWSZfQv8w&t=12s.

Shankar, Guha. "'People Who Stood Up': Mississippi Women in the Civil Rights Movement." *Folklife Today*, June 4, 2017. https://blogs.loc.gov/folklife/2017/06/standing-up-and-speaking-out-mississippi-women-in-the-civil-rights-movement/.

Smith, Beverly Jean. "The K–12 National Seeking Educational Equity and Diversity (SEED) Project: Teaching as a Political and Relational Act." *Women's Studies Quarterly* 28, no. 3/4 (2000): 137–53. http://www.jstor.org/stable/40005479.

"SNCC Leaves McComb." SNCC Digital Gateway. Duke University Libraries, July 14, 2020. https://snccdigital.org/events/sncc-leaves-mccomb/#:~:text=December%201961%20SNCC%20leaves%20McComb%20With%20most%20of,first%20voter%20registration%20effort%20had%20ground%20to%20halt.

Span, Christopher M. "'I Must Learn Now or Not at All': Social and Cultural Capital in the Educational Initiatives of Formerly Enslaved African Americans in Mississippi, 1862–1869." *The Journal of African American History* 87, no. 2 (2002): 196–205. https://doi.org/10.2307/1562463.

———. *From Cotton Field to Schoolhouse*. Chapel Hill: University of North Carolina Press, 2009.

———. "Post-Slavery? Post-Segregation? Post-Racial? A History of the Impact of Slavery, Segregation, and Racism on the Education of African Americans." *Teachers College Record: The Voice of Scholarship in Education* 117, no. 14 (2015): 53–74.

———. "Sam's Cottonfield Blues." *History of Education Quarterly* 62, no. 1 (2022): 10. https://doi.org/10.1017/heq.2021.53.

Span, Christopher M., and James D. Anderson. "The Quest for 'Book Learning': African American Education in Slavery and Freedom." *A Companion to African American History* (2004): 295–311. https://doi.org/10.1002/9780470996720.ch18.

Speer, Hugh W. *The Case of the Century: A Historical and Social Perspective on Brown v. Board of Education of Topeka, with Present and Future Implications*. Kansas City: University of Missouri-Kansas City, 1968.

St. Jean, Y., and J. R. Feagin. *Double Burden: Black Women and Everyday Racism*. Armonk, NY: M. E. Sharpe, 1998.

Stewart, James B. "Black/Africana Studies, Then and Now: Reconstructing a Century of Intellectual Inquiry and Political Engagement, 1915–2015." *The Journal of African American History* 100, no. 1 (2015): 87–118. https://doi.org/10.5323/jafriamerhist.100.1.0087.

Stewart, Joseph, Kenneth J. Meier, and Robert E. England. "In Quest of Role Models: Change in Black Teacher Representation in Urban School Districts, 1968–1986." *The Journal of Negro Education* 58, no. 2 (1989): 140–52. https://doi.org/10.2307/2295588.

Stewart, Robert, and the Smithsonian Institution. "Lonnie G. Bunch III." Smithsonian Institution. 2021. https://www.si.edu/about/bios/issis-g-bunch-iii.

Sturkey, William. *Hattiesburg: An American City in Black and White*. Cambridge: The Belknap Press of Harvard University Press, 2021.

Suitts, Steve. "Segregationists, Libertarians, and the Modern 'School Choice' Movement." *Southern Spaces* (2019). https://doi.org/10.18737/43330.2019.

Taylor, Jared. *Paved with Good Intentions: The Failure of Race Relations in Contemporary America*. New York: Carroll and Graf Publishers, 1993.

Terenzini, Patrick T., Alberto F. Cabrera, Carol L. Colbeck, Stefani A. Bjorklund, and John M. Parente. "Racial and Ethnic Diversity in the Classroom: Does It Promote Student Learning?" *The Journal of Higher Education* 72, no. 5 (2001): 509–31. https://doi.org/10.2307/2672879.

Terhune, C. P. "Coping in Isolation: The Experiences of Black Women in White Communities." *Journal of Black Studies* 38, no. 4 (2007): 547–64.

"The Importance of Windows and Mirrors in Stories." PBS, January 8, 2024. https://www.pbs.org/education/blog/the-importance-of-windows-and-mirrors-in-stories.

Thompson, Charles H. "The Status of Education of and for the Negro in the American Social Order." *The Journal of Negro Education* 8, no. 3 (1939): 489–521. https://doi.org/10.2307/2292646.

Thompson, Julius Eric. *Black Life in Mississippi: Essays on Political, Social, and Cultural Studies in a Deep South State*. Lanham, MD: University Press of America, 2001.

Thompson, Paul. *The Voice of the Past: Oral History*. Oxford: University Press, 2000.

———. "The Voice of the Past: Oral History." In Robert Perks, Alistair Thomson, Alex Haley, Alessandro Portelli, and Graham Smith, *The Oral History Reader*, 3rd ed., 34. London: Routledge/Taylor and Francis Group, 2016.

Till-Mobley, Mamie, and Christopher Benson. *Death of Innocence: The Story of the Hate Crime That Changed America*. New York: Random House, 2003.

Tillman, Linda C. "(Un)Intended Consequences of *Brown*." *Education and Urban Society* 36, no. 3 (2004): 280–303.

Todd-Breland, Elizabeth. *A Political Education: Black Politics and Education Reform in Chicago since the 1960s*. Chapel Hill: University of North Carolina Press, 2018.

Toppo, Greg. "Thousands of Black Teachers Lost Jobs." *USA Today*, April 28, 2004.

Toppo, Greg, and Mark Nichols. "Decades after Civil Rights Gains, Black Teachers a Rarity in Public Schools." *USA Today*, February 4, 2017. https://www.usatoday.com/story/news/nation-now/2017/02/01/decades-after-civil-rights-gains-black-teachers-rarity-public-schools/96721684/.

Trescott, Jacqueline. "Personal History: The African American Museum's Lonnie Bunch Looks Forward by Looking Back." *Washington Post*. October 17, 2005. https://www.washingtonpost.com/archive/lifestyle/2005/10/17/personal-history/bf759628-06a0-4605-9846-f3cd271a9c7e/.

Tucker, Shirley. *Mississippi from Within*. New York: Arco Publishing Co., 1965.

Turner, Kara Miles. "'Getting It Straight': Southern Black School Patrons and the Struggle for Equal Education in the Pre- and Post-Civil Rights Eras." *The Journal of Negro Education* 72, no. 2 (2003): 217–29. https://doi.org/10.2307/3211171.

Tushnet, Mark V. *The NAACP's Legal Strategy against Segregated Education, 1925–1950*. Chapel Hill: University of North Carolina Press, 2004.

United States Bureau of the Census. "1960 Census: Population, Volume I. Characteristics of the Population, Part 26 Mississippi." Washington DC: U.S. Government Printing Office, 1963.

United States Department of Education. "Racial/Ethnic Enrollment in Public Schools." National Center for Education Statistics. 2014. http://nces.ed.gov/programs/coe/indicator_cge.asp.

United States Department of Education. "US Department of Education—Condition of Education." National Center for Education Statistics. 2020.

Unknown. *School De-Segregation in Issaquena and Sharkey Counties*. 1960.

Van Den Bersselaar, Dmitri. "Imagining Home: Migration and the Igbo Village in Colonial Nigeria." *Journal of African History* 46, no. 1 (March 2005): 51–73. https://doi.org/10.1017/S0021853704000015.

Vansina, Jan. *Oral Tradition as History*. Madison: University of Wisconsin Press, 2014.

Waite, Cally L. "The Challenge of Teaching *Brown*." *History of Education Quarterly* 44, no. 1 (2004): 98–100.

Walker, Alice. "Those Who Love Us Never Leave Us Alone with Our Grief: Reading *Barracoon*." Alice Walker—The Official Website for American Novelist and Poet. March 31, 2018. https://alicewalkersgarden.com/2018/03/with-our-grief-reading-barracoon-the-story-of-the-last-black-cargo/.

Walker, Vanessa Siddle. *Their Highest Potential: An African American School Community in the Segregated South*. Chapel Hill: University of North Carolina Press, 1996.

———. "Valued Segregated Schools for African American Children in the South, 1935–1969: A Review of Common Themes and Characteristics." *Review of Educational Research* 70, no. 3 (2000): 253–85.

———. "African American Teaching in the South: 1940–1960." *American Educational Research Journal* 38, no. 4 (2001): 751–79.

———. "Black Educators as Educational Advocates in the Decades Before *Brown v. Board of Education*." *Educational Researcher* 42, no. 4 (2013): 207–22. http://www.jstor.org/stable/23462367.

———. "The 2014 Charles H. Thompson Lecture-Colloquium Presentation. School 'Outer-Gration' and 'Tokenism': Segregated Black Educators Critique the Promise of Education Reform in the Civil Rights Act of 1964." *The Journal of Negro Education* 84, no. 2 (2015): 111–24. https://doi.org/10.7709/jnegroeducation.84.2.0111.

———. *Lost Education of Horace Tate: Uncovering the Hidden Heroes Who Fought for Justice in Schools*. New York: New Press, 2018.

———. "Askwith Forums Black Educators and the Struggle for Justice in Schools." YouTube, March 29, 2019. https://www.youtube.com/watch?v=W8YDM7v8Few.

Watkins, W. H. *The White Architects of Black Education: Ideology and Power in America, 1865–1954*. New York: Teachers College Press, 2001.

Wells, Ida B., and Alfreda M. Duster. *Crusade for Justice*. Chicago: University of Chicago Press, 1970.

Wharton, Vernon Lane. *The Negro in Mississippi 1865–1890*. Chapel Hill: University of North Carolina Press, 1947.

Whitfield, Stephen J. *A Death in the Delta: The Story of Emmett Till*. Baltimore: Johns Hopkins University Press, 1991.

Wilkerson, Isabel. *Caste: The Origins of Our Discontents*. New York: Random House, 2021.

Williams, Heather Andrea. "'Clothing Themselves in Intelligence': The Freedpeople, Schooling, and Northern Teachers, 1861–1871." *The Journal of African American History* 87, no. 4 (2002): 372–89. https://doi.org/10.2307/1562471.

Williams, Heather Andrea. *Self-Taught: African American Education in Slavery and Freedom*. Chapel Hill: University of North Carolina Press, 2009.

Wilson, Reginald. "Recruiting and Retaining Minority Teachers." *The Journal of Negro Education* 57, no. 2 (1988): 195–97. https://doi.org/10.2307/2295449.

Wirt, Frederick M. *Politics of Southern Equality: Law and Social Change in a Mississippi County*. Chicago: Aldine Publishing Co., 1971.

Zamani-Gallaher, E. M., V. C. Polite, S. L. Graves, and T. N. Stevenson. "A Needle in a Haystack: The Search for African American Female Teachers in K–12 Education." In *African American Females Addressing Challenges and Nurturing the Future*, 79–102. Michigan State University Press, 2013.

Zinn, Howard. "Schools in Context: The Mississippi Idea." *Nation*. November 23, 1964.

Zirkel, Sabrina. "Ongoing Issues of Racial and Ethnic Stigma in Education 50 Years after *Brown v. Board*." *The Urban Review* 37, no. 2 (2005): 107–26. https://doi.org/10.1007/s11256-005-0004-4.

Index

Adam, Yolanda, 27
"African American Literature I," 113
African Americans: empowering Black identity in, 105–107; importance of Black spaces for, 95–98; importance of education to, 93–94; longstanding legacies of, 128–129; love as resistance and, 107–108; maintaining their agency and womanhood, 82–83; mentors and kinship among, 101–102; nurturing the whole child, 103–105; resilience of, 74–75; saving democracy, 88–89; sense of Black community among, 98–101; yearbooks and, 118–123. *See also* Black women educators
agency, Black women's, 82–83
All Your Selfish Ways, 109
Anderson, James, xxiv
Angelou, Maya, 27
"Annihilation No. 7–11," 110–111
Armstrong, Linda, 17, 45–50, 112, 117; on the Black community, 101; on importance of yearbooks, 118; on mentors, 102; on nurturing by her mother, 103
artifacts, 118–127
authors and activists, 50–57
Ayers v. Fordice, 22

Baker, Ella, 131
Banks, Stanley E., 110–111
Barracoon: The Story of the Last "Black Cargo," 92
Beard, Eileen, 54
Benson, Ariana, 12
Berrey, Stephen, 82, 83
Betts, Archie, 54
Black Boy, 4
Black Codes, 5
Black community, 98–101
Black Feminist Thought: Knowledge, Consciousness, and the Politics of Empowerment, 82
Black identity: empowering, 105–107; nurturing the whole child and, 104–105
Black spaces, 95–98
Black voice and activism, 83
Blackwell, Unita, 6
Black women educators: artifacts and relics of, 118–127; as authors and activists, 50–57; as a collective, 94–95; empowering Black identity, 105–107; future of, 132–133; histories of, xxiii–xxxi, 14–15; importance of Black spaces and, 95–98; legacies of, 115–117; loss of jobs due to desegregation, 132; mentors of,

Index

Black women educators (*continued*)
101–102, 112; in Mississippi, 4, 5;
nurturing the whole child, 103–105;
oral histories of (*see* oral histories);
as principals, 37–40, 58–64, 66–69;
protective spaces and, 86–88; as
school counselors, 26–28, 57–58; as
sociologists, 50–57; in special education, 40–44; student perspectives
on, 114–115; yearbooks and, 118–123.
See also African Americans
Bobbitt, Mary Lewis, 17, 40–44, 117;
on common goal of enriching the
Black community, 101; on experience of growing up in an all-Black
community, 99; on interactions
between white teachers and Black
students, 97–98
Bolton, Charles C., 6
Bonnette, Aliyah, xxxii, 129
Bracey, Glenn, 117
Brown, Julia, 17, 26–28, 117
Brown II decision, 85
Brown v. Board of Education, xxiv,
xxvi–xxviii, 2–3, 14, 64, 107; Bettie
Dahmer on, 22; desegregation after,
5–6; Joyce A. Ladner on, 50; resistance to, 3–4, 84–86; sense of Black
community prior to, 98–101; transformative impact of, 88–89
Bunch, Lonnie, xxiv, xxx, 15–17, 112;
on the importance of Black spaces,
98; Smithsonian Institution and,
18–20. *See also* oral histories
Burning Bridges, 11

"Cartography," 14
"Certain Swirl, A," xxxv
Chernoff, Maxine, 91
Civil Rights Act, 6
Civil Rights Movement, 115
Clifton, Lucille, 13, 15
Collins, Patricia Hill, 82, 84, 86
Collins, Phillip, xiv, xxxv
Congratulations Dr. Ladner, 131
Connor, Peggy Jean, 4
Contact #13, 90

Cooper, Charles, 17, 28–32, 117, 124; on
Black community, 99–100; impact
of, 114; on importance of yearbooks,
118, 119

Dahmer, Bettie, 17, 21–22, 114, 117
Dahmer, Ellie Jewell Davis, 4, 21, 22,
50, 71–74, 117
Dahmer, Vernon, 4, 21, 22, 50, 54
Davis, Trinity, 17
Demery, Kevin, 11
democracy, 88–89
De Priest, Oscar Stanton, 54
DePriest Herald, 118, 124–126
DePriest schools, 54, 118–128
desegregation/integration, 2–3, 22,
132; Barbara Elaine Jones on,
34–35; Eleanor Deloris Goins
on, 38; in the Forrest County and
Hattiesburg Public Schools, 87,
88; importance of Black spaces
and, 95–98; Jemye Heath on, 69;
Juruthin (Rosetta) Woullard on,
61–62; Katherine Fowler on, 65–66;
resistance to, 3–4, 84–86; sense of
Black community prior to, 98–101;
white schools privatized to stop,
85–86. *See also* segregation
Dozier, Helen, 119

Earl Travillion High School, 85, 88;
Barbara Elaine Jones and, 33;
Charles Cooper and, 30, 32, 121;
Eleanor Deloris Goins and, 40;
Joyce A. Ladner and, 50–51, 54;
Julia Brown and, 26–27; Katherine
Fowler and, 64–65; Linda Armstrong and, 45; yearbooks, 118–123
Easton, W. L., 84
Evers, Medgar, 4, 6, 50, 54
Evers, Myrlie, 6

Fairclough, Adam, xxv
Field, Kendra, 118
Fitch, Lynn, 22
FORDETRA, 17, 26–28, 59, 128
For My People, 80

Index

"For My People," 116
Forrest County Public Schools, 21–22, 28–32, 37, 45, 87, 88
Fowler, Katherine, 17, 64–66, 115, 116, 117; on nurturing the whole child, 104
Frankenberg, Erica, 133
Fultz, Michael, 85–86
Funchess, Glenda, 17

Givens, Jarvis, 3, 95–96
Glassie, Henry, xxvii
Goins, Eleanor Dolores, 17, 37–40, 94, 117; on empowering Black identity, 105–106; on nurturing the whole child, 104
Great Migration, 128

"Haint Blue," 93
Hale, Jon, 5, 102, 115
Hale-Green, Carolyn, 17, 57–58, 117; on empowering Black identity, 105; on nurturing the whole child, 105
Haley, Alex, 15
Hamer, Fannie Lou, 6, 138
Hardy, Harris, 8
Harris, Anthony, 17, 23–25
Hattiesburg, Mississippi, 8–9; Black community in, 99–100; map of, 7
Hattiesburg American, 3
Hattiesburg Public Schools, 23–25, 87, 88; legacies of teachers in, 115–117; teachers of, 94–95
Haw Contemporary Gallery, 19
Heath, Jemye, 14, 17, 66–69, 117
Highlights, 35
historians, Black, 18–20
Historically Black Colleges and Universities (HBCUs), 54–55
Hopkins, Kevin, xxvi, 1, 80, 92, 112, 131
Houck, Davis W., 4
Houston, Charles Hamilton, 107
Howard, Tyrone C., 99
Howard University, 54
Hughes, Kenny, 31
Hurston, Zora Neale, xxiii, xxvi, xxvii, 92

integration. *See* desegregation/integration
I've Got the Light of Freedom, xxvii–xxviii
I Wish the Rain Had Come That Day, 13

Jackson, Alpheus Bonard, 45
Jackson, Jesse, 36
Jackson, Zola, 30, 45, 51, 58, 60, 114, 123; dedication of, 81–82; involvement with the Black community, 100, 101; legacy of, 116; as mentor, 101; oral history of, 69–71
James, Jimmie, 119
Jim Crow South, xxviii–xxix, xxxi, 25, 82, 128, 132; Anthony Harris on, 24–25; Black families in, 82–84; Black voice and activism in, 83; Black women's agency in, 82–84; interactions between white teachers and Black students in, 97–98; love as resistance in, 107–108; lynchings in, 4–5; protective spaces in, 86–88; sense of Black community, 98–101
Jones, Ashley M., 113, 138
Jones, Barbara Elaine, 17, 33–36, 114–115, 117
Joyce, Mario, xv, xxvi, xxxiv, xxxvi, 109, 139
Junior National Association for the Advancement of Colored People (NAACP), 40, 42

Kelley, Robin, xxviii–xxx
Kennard, Clyde, 54, 101
"Killing Emmett," 4
Killingsworth, JC, 38
King, Martin Luther, Jr., 36
kinship, 101–102
KKK, 36

Ladner, Joyce A., xxvii, xxviii, 17, 21, 112, 114, 116, 117; as civil rights leader, 101; on empowering Black identity, 106–107; encouraged as

Ladner, Joyce A. (*continued*)
  a child, 93; on how her mother taught her, 82–83; oral history of, 50–57; on resilience of Black educators, 87–88
Lange, Dorothea, 1
Lê, Hùng, 13
legacies of Black women educators, 115–117
"Lessons," 81
Lewis, Earl, xxix
Light Change, A, 139
Lost Women, The, 13
love as resistance, 107–108
"Love Poem in the Black Field," 12
lynchings, 4–5

Magnitude of Us: An Educator's Guide to Creating Culturally Responsive Classrooms, The, xxvii
Manning, Alva, 17, 117; on empowering Black identity, 105
Marimutu, Rebecca, xxvi, 76, 90
Marshall, Nate, 77–79
Marshall, Thurgood, 107
mentors, 101–102
Mentors, 112
Midnight Rivers, xxxii
Milner, Richard, 99
"Miss Banks," 91
Mississippi: Black families in Jim Crow, 82–84; Hattiesburg, 7, 8–9; historical context of, 2–3; importance of history of, 9–10; longstanding legacies of, 128–129; lynchings in, 4–5; opposition to desegregation in, 3–4; resistance to *Brown* in, 84–86; White Citizens' Council in, 85
"Mississippi Goddam," 1, 4

National Association for the Advancement of Colored People (NAACP), 50, 67, 71, 85, 115
National Association of Colored Women (NACW), 85
Noonan, Martha Prescod Norman, 133

nurturing networks, 84

"On Caskets," 77–79
oral histories, 14–17, 132; Armstrong, Linda, 45–50; Bobbitt, Mary Lewis, 40–44; Brown, Julia, 26–28; Bunch, Lonnie, 18–20; Cooper, Charles, 28–32; Dahmer, Bettie, 21–22; Dahmer, Ellie, 71–74; demonstrating the dedication of educators, 81–82; Fowler, Katherine, 64–66; Goins, Eleanor Deloris, 37–40; Hale-Green, Carolyn, 57–58; Harris, Anthony, 23–25; Heath, Jemye, 66–69; Jones, Barbara Elaine, 33–36; Ladner, Joyce A., 50–57; Woullard, Juruthin (Rosetta), 58–64
Oral History Reader, The, 16

Parent Teacher Association (PTA), 64, 124
Payne, Charles, xxvii–xxviii, 15
Pettit, Emily, 14
"Place for Fire, A," 130
Plessy v. Ferguson, 2, 102
Portelli, Alessandro, 16
principals, 37–40, 58–64, 66–69
protective spaces, 86–88

race women, 54–55
Rankine, Claudia, 134–137
relics, 118–127
Resistance Begins at Home: The Black Family and Lessons in Survival and Subversion in Jim Crow Mississippi, 83
Roots, 15
Ross, Barbara, 17, 117
Ruefle, Mary, xxxiv, xxxv

Scarborough, Ed, 31
school counselors, 26–28, 57–58
second-class citizenship, 84
segregation, 2–3; Charles Cooper on benefits of, 29–30; empowering Black identity during, 106–107;

Joyce A. Ladner on, 50–52; Juruthin (Rosetta) Woullard on, 62–63; Linda Armstrong on, 46–48. *See also* desegregation
"Segregation Is Constitutional but Compulsory Integration Is Unconstitutional," 84
"separate but equal" doctrine, 2
Shockley, Evie, 2
Siddle Walker, Vanessa, xxiv, 94–95, 96–97, 132; on empowering Black identity, 105; on mentors, 102; on nurturing the whole child, 104
Silencing the Past, Power, and the Production of History, 83
Simone, Nina, 1, 4
Smith, Freddye, 17, 117
Smith, Jeanette, 4
Smithsonian Institution, 18–19
sociologists, 50–57
"Some Years There Exists a Wanting to Escape," 134–137
Span, Christopher M., xix–xx, xxiv, xxx, xxxiii, 9, 74–75, 88–89, 98, 107–108, 112, 128–129
special education educators, 40–44
Static Field, xxxvi
statistical haiku (or, how do they discount us? let me count the ways), 2
Stempleman, Jordan, 81, 130

Student Nonviolent Coordinating Committee (SNCC), 8, 37, 50, 115, 133
Sturkey, William, 9, 82, 95, 117
Swensen, Cole, 93

Taransky, Michelle, 140–141
Their Eyes Were Watching God, xxvi
They Just Want a Sip from Your Water, 129
Thompson, Paul, 16
Ties That Bind, The, 106
Till, Emmett, 6, 22
Tougaloo College, 27
Travillion Tiger Boosters, 122
Trouillot, Michel-Rolph, 83

Walker, Margaret, 80, 116
Washington Post, 19
Wells, Ida B., 6, 22, 54–55
"What If I Told You, He Grew Up," 140–141
Wheatley, Phillis, xxvi
White Citizens' Council, 85
Woullard, Juruthin (Rosetta), 17, 58–64, 96, 117
Wright, Richard, 4

yearbooks, 118–123

Dr. Marlee Bunch, educator, author. Photo by Reckless Robot Photography.

DR. MARLEE BUNCH is an interdisciplinary educator, scholar, and author. Her research examines the oral histories of Black female educators in Hattiesburg, Mississippi, who taught between 1954 and 1970, and the implications that desegregation had for their lives. She received her doctoral degree from the University of Illinois in 2022 in Education/Policy/Organizational Leadership, with a concentration in Diversity/Equity/Inclusion. Additionally, she has a master's degree in education (MEd), a master's degree in Gifted Education (MS), a bachelor's degree in English, a certification in English as a Second Language (ESL), a teaching certification, and a certificate in Diversity/Equity/Inclusion. She was awarded a National Academy of Education/Spencer Postdoctoral Fellowship in 2025.

Her publications include *The Magnitude of Us: An Educator's Guide to Creating Culturally Responsive Classrooms* (2024) and *Leveraging AI for Human-Centered Learning: Culturally Responsive and Social-Emotional Classroom Practice in Grades 6–12* (2025). Bunch is the founder of the un/HUSH teaching framework. In her free time, she enjoys collecting art, reading, spending time with family and friends, and attempting to beat her six-year-old at Hi Ho Cherry O. You can learn more about her work at https://www.marleebunch.com/.

Utē Pettit, *Swamp Sunflowers*, 2022. Photograph. "My work envisions a Black, Indigenous territory where we are returning to a deeply symbiotic relationship with the earth. In my recent work I'm specifically focusing on regions we currently call louisiana & Misi-Ziibi, as my ancestry is of these lands. My grandfather is actually from the Hattiesburg area (Laurel). He and my grandmother were educators in Marion County, just 30 minutes away from Hattiesburg. I feel excited for my work to support your research, as it's very much of relation to my own family history in Mississippi. I've been interested in the role Black southern women have played in holding our communities together, from forming cooperatives to holding quilting bees, to being medicine women, educators, farmers, juke joint owners and entertainers."

The University of Illinois Press
is a founding member of the
Association of University Presses.

Composed in 10.5/13 Mercury Text
with Avenir display
by Jim Proefrock
at the University of Illinois Press
Manufactured by Sherican Books, Inc.

University of Illinois Press
1325 South Oak Street
Champaign, IL 61820-6903
www.press.uillinois.edu